Tantı

Please note the information contained within this document is for educational and entertainment purposes only. All effort has been executed to present accurate, up to date, reliable, complete information. No warranties of any kind are declared or implied. Readers acknowledge that the author is not engaging in the rendering of legal, financial, medical or professional advice. The content within this book has been derived from various sources. Please consult a licensed professional before attempting any techniques outlined in this book.

By reading this document, the reader agrees that under no circumstances is the author responsible for any losses, direct or indirect, that are incurred as a result of the use of information contained within this document, including, but not limited to, errors, omissions, or inaccuracies.

Table of Contents

Introduction: What Makes Tantric Sex Different and Unique

Most spiritual traditions that have been practiced for thousands of years have been ignored due to modern medicine and technologies. This has been evident in instances such as eroticism and sexuality. Others have been repressed and condemned without further interest to learn about them. Many of these sacred activities have been received with toughness. It's not uncommon to hear how spiritual traditions are unwelcomed for a good part of society. Performing any of these might seem primitive or not advanced for many, despite the fact that the purposes of such practices are for the continuation of life.

A few of those condemning traditional practices have been concerned with the doctrines that deal with the human spirit- i.e. principles that considered sexual enjoyment as a way of achieving balance, life fulfillment, and spiritual elevation.

Tantra is one of such traditional practices. What is fundamental to understanding Tantra is its own parameters, its nature, and its holistic scope. Tantra is a tradition of oriental origin (from India, specifically). In Western societies, tantric sex has been almost synonymous with techniques for controlling ejaculation. It is true that Tantra advises how to delay ejaculation in order for the couple to enjoy a carnal and spiritual union. Not only in terms of time, but also regarding the pleasure of the encounter. However, tantric sex does not end there. Tantric sex can benefit a person or a couple well beyond sexual pleasure.

Tantra preaches the cultivation of sexuality during and outside the sexual act itself. Also, it encourages us to live in an erotic way every moment we share with our partner. Regarding sex, it has the status of a spiritual ritual and it's called maithuna. Due to the aforementioned reason, Tantra teaches sex positions–as well as different methods of foreplay, such as kissing and caressing that lovers can perform on each other. All of this works together with what is known as erogenous zones. Tantra deals with sexual rituals where the divine is filtered in the carnal act, allowing lovers to flow to other planes of existence. Of course, it also considers different techniques to control ejaculation–although it's not its central focus.

Outside of the realm of sexuality, Tantra can also help you in other aspects of your life such as:

- Erotic massages techniques that have been tailored to stimulate and relax the energy flow of lovers by raising awareness of bodily sensations.

- Similar to that, it's also concerned with sexual acupressure, which is concentrated on stimulating the erogenous zones.

- Traditional foods that have aphrodisiac effects.

- Curating a good atmosphere that can help you to potentiate your sexual life.

- Tantric dances and music as an alternative of foreplay

The central part of Tantra are body movements, which are used to feed our inner energy. Finally, for advanced practitioners, tantrism offers a series of erotic rituals proffered to the ancient Indian gods and a series of group sex practices.

The true secret of tantric eroticism is to think of sex as both a special and ritual ceremony. To fully enjoy it, you have to prepare all the steps in detail and spend some time beforehand to prepare internally for the moment of the sexual encounter. Within the logic of Tantra, sex is just another piece of a life well lived.

While it's not easy to summarize what sex implies from a Tantric point of view, there are two crucial aspects that are needed to be understood:

- For one, that the body is a temple of divinity from the tantric perspective. In this sense, the sexual union is only the first step on the road to cosmic unity with what is considered as divine in the Indian culture. Sex is a small-scale representation of the law of attraction of the universe and, more specifically, a human reproduction of the erotic embrace between the goddess Shakty and the god Shiva.

- Second, sex is the unity of a man and a woman. Under such logic, every man has Shiva inside of him, while every woman has Shakty inside of her. The sexual ritual of maithuna is the earthly representation of the fusion that exists between these two gods in the transcendental plane. Furthermore, the main purpose of the sexual union between man and woman is to achieve the innate ecstasy of the divine.

With all, Tantra manages to provide us with joy and fulfillment because we're addressing the body in its divine essence. Respect and attention should be the central values of true tantrism. Moreover, love is to drive encounters between women and men to achieve its purpose.

Nothing is further from the tantric understanding of sex than rushing and forcing. The sacred ritual of maithuna requires hours of commitment that are devoted to pleasure. Sexual gratifications are a slow process that can have highly rewarding outcomes if done properly. Although techniques to delay ejaculation are possible if you start to practice Tantra, try to make the most of the many tips we're going to address in this book. Likewise, bear in mind that penetration in Tantric sex is a step and not a goal to achieve.

This said, read this book carefully. If possible, make sure that your partner is on-board and willing to put into practice the advice I'm sharing here with you. This is a beautiful and sensual path that is full of caresses, kisses, sweet words, smells, sensations, foods and drinks, which will help you to replenish energy and fluids.

Therefore, enjoy this journey as you learn about Tantra and put   in   practice.

Chapter 1: Benefits of Tantric Sex: How Can it Benefit a Couple's Sexual Life

As explained in the introduction, Tantra is the application of tantric techniques during the sexual union. The key is to feel how energy flows from the center of the body to the genital organs and travels throughout your body. Tantric sex includes the practice of various meditation and yoga exercises to learn how to flow energy into the body and into your partner. The idea is to achieve a balance between the male and female energy. It is the sexual union that honors creation and equilibrium.

Because of this, there are several benefits of practicing tantric sex. Some of them are as follows:

Tantra Expands Your Chances of Loving
Tantric sex shows you how to achieve a psychological and spiritual connection with your partner. It also teaches you to love yourself.

Helps You to Have a Healthier Lifestyle

Breathing techniques allow more oxygen to reach your body. Not to say that tantric exercises and postures strengthen your muscles. There are direct links between the effects produced by relaxation, meditation, and spirituality in the improvement of emotional health. People who are more spiritual have a more controlled blood pressure, as well as less of a chance of suffering anxiety and depression. It also helps to keep hormonal changes stable and improves the immune system.

It Can Help You to Stay Young

In addition to the contributions mentioned above, tantric sex also makes you feel younger, vigorous, and happy.

It Empowers Women

Many women suffer from low self-esteem, and have a poor image of their body, meaning that they do not enjoy sex at all. The macho practices that continue, unfortunately, in certain sectors of society make a woman feel like an object to give pleasure rather than as part of a pleasant experience. In tantric sex, the woman is treated with respect and love. For the man who practices tantric sex, it is an honor to be with his partner.

It Empowers Man

Many men worry and have complexes due to society's expectations. Often, there is strong pressure regarding sexual performance, the size of the penis or even erectile dysfunctions. Many men do not really know how to please their partners. With tantra, man acquires confidence and dares to experience new horizons within the relationship. Tantra opens their minds.

Helps to Achieve Real Satisfaction During Sex

When sex ends, many people feel as if the act was incomplete. This is very frequent because the sexual act is not only genital. If sexual encounters are only focused on penetration or stimulation of the penis or vagina, an orgasm might have been achieved, but without a real connection. Hearts are touched through tantric sex due to shared energy. You can feel the inside of your partner beyond the body. When this type of union occurs, both body and mind are fed.

Relieves Anxiety and Depression

A good number of men and women in the world suffer from anxiety and depression. Some symptoms that are often experienced are fatigue, languor, sleep disorders, and eating problems. With tantric sex, you will remove everything that torments you and fill your channels with new and pure energy.

Increases the Number of Times You Have Sex

When you raise sex to a sacred level, it takes you on a richer dimension. Sex becomes a more emotional act, not only physical.

Prolongs the Pleasure

Tantric techniques to make love help people to last longer during their encounters. Men will have better ejaculatory control, both learning to bring sexual energy to any part of the body and turn it into spiritual manifestations.

Heals the Wounds of the Past

Tantric sex can help overcome traumatic experiences, especially cases of sexual and physical abuse. In Tantra, the sexual experience is sacred and respectful, which helps to overcome psychological barriers. Thus, it's very useful to remove the general fears of facing life.

Deepens Your Connection With Others

Tantra sex gives life more meaning and enriches your relationship with your partner.

Affects Your World in a Positive Way

You will have more strength to achieve your personal goals. The energy of love is noticeable and extends to everything around you. It can even alter the energy of the planet, taking into account that we are all connected on a metaphysical level.

Chapter 2: Getting prepared for Tantric Sex – The Importance of Energy and Chakras

Within Tantra, there are two basic notions to be comprehended: Kundalini energy (simply referred to as Kundalini) and the chakras. Both are essential to be prepared for tantric sex because they help us to understand it in its full and true meaning. Once you've fully understood them, it will be much easier for you to follow with all that we'll discuss in the following chapters.

Kundalini Energy

Because tantric sex is a highly enjoyable and fulfilling experience, it traditionally has had a very concrete function. This is to allow the Kundalini energy to ascend from the lower chakras to the superior ones. This way, it makes possible the expansion and ascension of all the planes of the human being: corporal, spiritual, psychic, and energetic. However, before going further in this subject, you might be asking yourself what Kundalini is and what makes it different to the chakras?

First, the Kundalini is a psychosexual and sacred energy. Think of it as a kind of "sacred spark" that exists inside of your body. It can also be described as a sort of engine for the human being. Kundalini plays a key role because it is an energy that the body needs to revitalize the natural cycles of cell generation. It's also fundamental for other processes, such as for the expansion of the spirit to higher ends. The easiest way to understand it is to think about it as what we commonly refer as the libido–while it doesn't mean exactly that.

It's often thought that its presence is limited, especially for those people who haven't been acquainted with this concept. Nevertheless, it has a huge potential and people who have never utilized it might have a huge reserve inside them. Not using the Kundalini can have a negative effect on you. However, once you start to mobilize and instrumentalize it, you will start to feel full of energy.

Indian cultures tend to represent the Kundalini as a sleeping snake that is coiled on itself. In Sanskrit language, the term kundall means "rolled up."

Within this concept, it's located near the base of your spine. As you will realize later, this means that you can find it in your first chakra.

The idea of Kundalini is to "wake up" the snake and make it ascend through the chakras. This means that you'll start a path toward fullness in every way and toward a final lighting. In this sense, when the Kundalini arises and starts ascending toward the chakras, raising up each one of them revitalizes your capabilities and full potential in sexual and non-sexual ways. Maithuna is just one of the means to achieve this. This means the fulfillment of sexual encounters according to tantric precepts.

The ultimate goal of the tantric search is the journey of the Kundalini through the chakras. This is about making it move from the primitive animality of the first three chakras (which are linked to survival, sex, and food) toward the ones concerned with advanced human matters, i.e. the fourth and the fifth chakra, which are related to love and creation.

When the journey is completed and upon reaching the sixth and seventh chakra, it arrives at the cosmic and divine level. Maithuna or tantric carnal union is one of the ways to make that cosmic trip. The chakras we have mentioned before are the preceding topic for Kundalini energy.

However, you might be asking yourself what the Chakras are. These are the seven energy centers found in the human body that are in line with the so-called central channel. Each is related to different aspects of life and manage a particular energy that's transmitted to the rest of the body.

Muladhara: First Chakra

Its name means "root" or "support" and is located at the base of the spine between the anus and the genitals. Basically, it is the central energy where the fundamental material for survival resides. This chakra influences all the earthly aspects and is linked to two primary and inescapable sides of any existence: physical security and survival. Muladhara connects us with aspects such as health, hygiene, home, food, money, and material goods.

Svadhisthana: Second Chakra

The meaning of its name is "the proper dwelling" and is located in the coccyx. It is the seat of rebirth and the awakening of consciousness, and encourages the search and encounter of meaningful relationships. It's related to sensuality, pleasure, and eroticism. Furthermore, it's the first step on the path that takes the human being beyond what is considered strictly material.

Manipura: Third Chakra

This is considered to be the route of the mystical and transforming fire. Manipura, whose name means "city of joy" or "city of jewels," is the sun chakra, or the chakra of light and abundance. It's the most important vital energy center of the human being. Within it resides will, power, and the emotions. It's located in the middle between the naval and the pit of the stomach.

Anahatha: Fourth Chakra

It means "undefeated" or "not beaten" and is located in the dorsal region behind the heart. It corresponds to the energy center of the chest and marks the birth of a higher understanding. Anahatha is, likewise, the spiritual birth and is linked to compassion, tenderness and solidarity while representing the desire for emotional unity and effectiveness.

Vishuddha: Fifth Chakra

It constitutes the starting point of good fortune and great liberation. It is located behind the throat and is the center of creativity and communication. It also constitutes the core of our devotion, since from there it is possible to connect with the divinity or any other form of the transcendent. Its name means "the big one" or "the pure one."

Ajna: Sixth chakra

Because it is located between the eyebrows, it is also known as "third eye." However, Ajna means the "command center" or "the one that directs." Ajna is the core of our logic and the true understanding of reality. Also, it's decisive in the search engine for spiritual love and authentic wisdom. It is also linked to concentration, imagination, fantasy, inspiration, and inner vision.

Sahasrara: Seventh Chakra

It is the highest energy vortex and is located outside the physical body, in a magnetic center that is above the front head. Sahasrara means "thousand petal lotus" or "crown chakra." When reaching the seventh and last chakra, Kundalini ends its way and this duality returns to a unity, thereby creating a sort of hyperconsciousness that is beyond spatial and temporary understanding. Due to this reason, it is there that a process of verification happens between the personality we have and our highest selves. Sahasrara is the site of inspiration, enlightenment, cosmic consciousness, and final realization.

Pleasure Areas

When the emotional component is very high, any touch, kissing, licking or biting of any part of the body can result in a powerful sexual stimulation. This is because the entire body can be an erotic zone if you receive contact from someone who is sexually attractive and desirable. However, the truth is that certain parts of your body are particularly sexually sensitive. These areas are often called erogenous zones, and their sensitivity is due to the rich network of nerve terminations. In a sexual circumstance, tactile or buccal stimulation in these areas become the first step to stimulate the whole body.

The discovery and exploration of the couple's erogenous zones must be affectionate and loving at all times and not simply mechanical. Every woman and every man should try to discover everything possible about the body of their partners. Both must learn to get excited slowly, but at a steady pace to gradually discover which parts of the body are more pleasurable.

The Male Erogenous Zones

Most of the male's erogenous zone is located in the genitals. The entire genital area of the male body responds to the slightest touch, and there are many specific points to be explored. The area just behind the basis of the penis (between it and the anus) that covers the prostate is exceptionally sensitive to touch–both during and erection as well as when reaching an orgasm. The testicles are extremely sensitive, and they should be handled gently. Otherwise, it can result in pain.

Without a doubt, however, the penis or lingam (as it is known in tantric sex) is the most sensitive erogenous zone, since that is where the most intense sensations are provoked and where pleasure is concentrated. The entire lingam is very sensitive, but the end of the glans are particularly rich in nerve endings, especially in its head. This is why it will react very quickly to minimum stimulation. The frenulum is also extremely sensitive in all men, just like the area behind the opening of the penis.

But given how sensitive it is, what characterizes the most the areas just mentioned is the speed by which a man can reach a level of excitement. This can predispose men in a full manner for the sexual act. Therefore, it's necessary for women to leave the genital area for last and begin stimulating men in other body parts that are also sensitive. Some of them are the following:

- The neck, ears, and eyelids

- The chest, especially the nipples

- The palm of the hands, although not usually an obvious erotic zone, responds very favorably to stimuli

- The back is an erogenous area

- The anus and the entire surrounding

The Female Erogenous Zones

Unlike its male counterpart, the entire woman's skin is an erogenous zone that will respond to friction, caresses, and kisses. However, there are certain areas where simulation can cause actual excitation. Some body parts are more intense in comparison to men.

The first and most important erogenous zone for women is the yoni–which is the female genitalia in tantric language. As well as with men, it's not convenient to reach it at the beginning of lovemaking. However, the reason for this is different for men. In the case of the male, the convenience of this delay lies in not achieving early over excitation. In the case of women, it is just the opposite. Since it takes longer to get excited, it doesn't react in the best way if the yoni is touched and caressed from the very beginning.

One of the reasons why caresses are so powerful and are enjoyed so much by women is that they excite and relax them. This prepares them for intercourse. For women, coitus is only welcome when she feels willing and has had enough stimulation. Her Yoni requires to lubricated and dilated to receive the lingam. Without the opportunity to raise the level of sex hormones through the kiss and, above all, the caresses, intercourse can be very uncomfortable for her.

Before reaching the genitals, the female body needs to be stimulated as follow:

- All kinds of erotic touch are highly stimulating for the head, including the forehead, eyebrows, eyelids and cheeks.

- The mouth is an erogenous zone of fundamental importance, since it produces a direct effect on the excitation of the genital organs.

- The earlobes are also highly stimulating.

- The neck, especially its back, responds strongly to stimulation.

- Armpits, hands, back, hips, and lower abdomen

- Breasts are erogenous to a high degree, especially the nipples.

- The area around the belly button is another primary area.

- The inner side of the thighs is highly sensitive to erotic stimuli.

- The anus and the entire surrounding area is particularly sensitive.

When the woman has reached a degree of excitement, then the lover can focus his attention her genitals. A highly erotic area is the perineum, which is an area of skin located between the entrance of the vagina and the anus. Both the major lips like the labia minora are also sectors that are rich in nerve endings and constitute an erogenous zone of great importance.

The latter are especially sensitive along their surface inside, in the cleft of the vulva. However, the clitoris is the body part with the greatest sexual sensitivity among women and the easiest to stimulate if the man learns to do it gently, skillfully, and without precipitation. However, and above everything else, proper lubrication, either from vaginal discharge or from saliva, is fundamental. If lubrication is insufficient, precisely because of its large number of nerve endings, the clitoris becomes irritated and the (otherwise) pleasant sensations become unpleasant.

The Clitoris: the Crown Jewel

The clitoris is an organ of the female body whose only function is providing pleasure, awakening eroticism and bioenergy, lighting the sexual fire, and powerfully raise the Kundalini energy.

Many of the millennial understandings of tantric sex refer to the clitoris as "the jewel in the crown" and in the oriental sexual tradition is revered, it should be respected and stimulated with both fingers and tongue. This in the sake that energy travels like electricity through the body and, with it, start the clital energy feedback known as "tantric circle."

The clitoris is located at the upper junction of the lips minors. The body of this organ has a back, a base, and an anterior part. When the woman is excited, the glans can swell to double its volume. When it reaches its highest degree of excitement and is close to orgasm, the entire clitoris retracts inward and downward, in the direction of the vagina, until it's central part is completely hidden.

The G Spot

Both women and men have in their genital organs a pleasure point called the "G spot." This is located behind the pubic bone, in the anterior wall of the vagina, along the urethra and its touch is similar to a lightweight relief button. It swells through sexual stimulation, when it goes from being the size of a chickpea to that of a nut. The best way to locate it is to insert one or two fingers somewhat bent above and make a movement similar to the gesture of "come here."

Men also have their own G-spot. This is in the anus at about 5 cm from the entrance, and its upper cavity is also watered by nerve endings similar to those of the female body. Stimulating it is a fundamental step on the road to pleasure and fulfillment sexually for both men and women–allowing the energy that lives in each one of them to flow freely and manifest.

The Fluids of Love

Since the love game begins first with kisses and caresses and ends with full sexual satisfaction, both the woman's body and the body of man expel a series of fluids that tantrism considers sacred. These are a kind of nectar of the gods. Basically, they can be divided into two groups: those tending to lubricate the genitals and those which are expelled as a result of orgasm.

Female Lubrication

For maithuna to develop fully, it is extremely important that there is lubrication before any attempt at penetrating. A good part of the natural lubrication of yoni is assured by the increase in the usual physiological secretion of the Bartholin glands. These glands emanate a clear secretion that is liquid and somewhat viscous. When this fluid comes in enough quantity, it then works as an excellent natural lubricant that has several advantages. For one, it does not only prevent irritation, but allows the lingam to enter into the yoni smoothly and decreases both male and female sensitivity.

Another source of lubrication is the glands of the cervix, which is a tip of the womb that emerges at the bottom of the yoni. Last but not least, there's also the humidification reactions of sexual arousal, known with the name of "vaginal transudation," consisting of an acidic liquid of light and milk-like color.

Male Lubrication

During the sexual arousal phase and before ejaculation, the man secretes a few drops of a fluid that appears at the tip of the lingam. This is sometimes referred to as the pre-seminal fluid. It has a consistency quite similar to the female lubrication fluid and is produced by the Cowper glands, which are located on each side of the urethra. Although is quite similar to the female lubrication fluid, men don't normally produce as much as women, and it is not enough for sexual encounters. Thus, it's necessary for women to lubricate as well to avoid discomfort.

Artificial Lubrication

If after performing foreplay the woman's lubrication isn't enough, it is necessary to ask yourself what the cause of such deficiency might be. Ask yourself why hasn't your body reacted to kisses and caresses? Is there any erogenous zone that has not received enough stimulation? Is there a problem of some other type (e.g. emotional) that blocks your sexual arousal?

There are periods in which the yoni is unable to produce enough lubricant to facilitate penetration–e.g. menopause, age, delay of sexual arousal, etc. Therefore, it can become necessary to use artificial lubricants to cover this function. However, be mindful that you just have to resort to them when all other attempts to emulate natural lubrication haven't been successful.

The first-choice product to be used is really important. In the past, any type of fatty substance of animal origin was used from animal or mineral that was at hand, which could generate irritation and even greater health problems. Butter and vaseline also fulfilled this role, and they were better options because they not only were effective, but they caused no irritation. Its disadvantage lies in the fact that they usually leave stains on the bedding.

At present, the market offers a whole series of products specifically designed to facilitate vulvar and vaginal lubrication. Ask a health provider to advise you about over-the-counter lubricants. Based on your needs and desires, you can opt for water-based or silicone-based lubricants. For some women, they might opt to take a low-dose of prescription estrogen that works to provide vaginal lubrication.

Semen

Semen is the name of the whitish fluid produced by the male genitals and containing all the necessary elements for human reproduction. Basically, this is suspended sperm in the seminal fluid. Ejaculation, as the emission of semen, is therefore a function that doesn't always come with orgasms. Orgasm may occur without ejaculation, as well as ejaculation without orgasm. Nevertheless, both usually take place simultaneously.

Orgasms consists of the crisis and the sudden relief of sexual tension, which is usually accompanied by the emission of semen. However, "dry orgasms" can also occur–which is the relief of sexual tension without ejaculatory emission. Sexual anhedonia is the opposite case, in which there's ejaculation without orgasms. Its main characteristic is the lack of pleasure when ejaculating. In other words, it is the lack of the psychophysical component of orgasm at the time of semen emission. This is a not a very frequent disorder. Nonetheless, it usually appears when there is some sort of psychiatric depression or other symptoms, such as fatigue or stress.

The role of semen in tantra is crucial. From a tantric point of view, semen is a source of energy. Thus, it's fundamental that such source is never wasted or misused. When a man has frequent ejaculations, there's a chance that he can feel weak or tired much of the time. Hence, tantra suggest a number of ways to control ejaculation and make the most out of semen.

Erotic Games with Semen

Because of its symbolism, semen can be used in several ways in tantra. For example, semen can be used as a fluid and as a lubricant for erotic massages. In such cases, a possibility is to have a seminal discharge on the female breasts or abdomen. Afterward, this can be spread with light movements on those and other areas. It also lends itself to games such as the following: make a fellatio until achieving ejaculation and, immediately, offer it to your partner in a sperm kiss. It can also be used as a lubricant to practice anal sex. And, of course, swallowing it usually constitutes for many men a type of proof of love from their partner.

It is impossible to describe the taste and smell of semen because this depends largely on the diet of the man and other variables of personal nature. Despite this, in broad strokes, it can be said that semen is presented as a slightly viscous liquid with a temperature a couple of degrees higher than that of the body. In most cases, the taste is bittersweet and has an aroma that vaguely reminds one of mint or in other cases can be similar to the sap of some fruit plants.

This is because one of the key components of semen is fructose–a sugar found in fruit. Another important component is ascorbic acid, which can be found in citrus and other fresh fruits. Among other components of semen are glucose and some proteins. However, ingestion of this fluid hardly causes weight gain. To do so, you would have to ingest very large amounts on a daily basis. Although, because ejaculation normally comes in small amounts, it's difficult to assess what effects it can cause at large.

The Female "Semen"

Not much is known about feminine ejaculation yet. In some women, in addition to the vaginal lubrication fluid, a fluid is released through the urethra at the time of sexual intercourse if the woman does have an orgasm. This feminine ejaculation occurrence depends highly on each woman. There are women who can ejaculate every time they have sex. Others rarely do. Some women can have multiple orgasms during one sexual encounter, although some experts suggest it occurs in only a small percentage of women. Many (perhaps most) do not even know that this bodily function exists in their bodies. In some cases, only stimulation of the G-spot induces to an ejaculatory orgasm. In others, clitoral stimulation is also needed.

For a long time, women who experienced feminine ejaculation went to the doctor worried that they were suffering from urinary incontinence. Many doctors, in their ignorance, recommended treatments for this "illness." But the liquid they were referring to was not urine. Physically and chemically speaking, it is far from the characteristics of urine. The outflow of fluid only occurs during sexual intercourse without the need for physical effort, and the aroma of secretion does not have that particular smell that urine has. Most women who ejaculate realize that the color of this fluid is not yellow; it is clear and odorless.

Chapter 3: Tantric Massages and Meditation: Lingam and Yoni Breathing

Within Tantra, sensual and loving massages practiced on a daily basis are a fundamental part of connecting with your partner. At those intermediate moments (which in no way must inevitably conclude in a sexual encounter if the couple does not want it), massages play a transcendental role. This is because it allows the awakening and unblocking of body sensations and unlocks energy in one or more points of the body. At the same time, it generates a very particular type of communication between the couple based on service and physical pleasure, which doesn't necessarily has to have an erotic purpose.

These exchanges generated by the massages are intended mainly to relax and stimulate the energy flow between lovers. As well as to stimulate every day the ability to give and enjoy during maithuna of an infinitely more satisfying and deep way.

The Couple During the Massage

For each partner to cherish each other during sessions of tantric massage and can perform massages in a holistic way, you must comply with certain rules and requirements. First and foremost, you should be aware that a massage session will be worthless if it is performed in a hurried manner and with the concentration placed, for example, in things unrelated to the moment.

The member of the couple who occupies the active role (that is, the one giving the massage) should:

- Free their mind of any thought or desire that concern any type of sexual gratification.

- Focus exclusively on the therapeutic power of the hands.

- Set aside worries, whatever is the nature of these. The massage requires the participant to "be here and now."

- Direct the intention and attention only at the service of the healing and pleasure of the other.

- Keep in mind that the more internally and physically relaxed is the one giving the massage, the greater the flow of healing energies and harmonizers will be transferred to the recipient.

- Synchronize breathing with that of your partner.

- In turn, the partner who plays a passive role (that is, the one who receives the massage) should:

- Be willing to accept and enjoy the pleasure that its partner is providing–without thinking that you are going toward a goal or objective (especially of a sexual nature)

- Rest your mind and get rid of all worries or thoughts that are unrelated to the moment.

- Warn if any movement or stimulus is uncomfortable or unpleasant so that your partner does not continue with it.

Convenient Posture

An enjoyable and comfortable position (for both members participating in the massage session) is essential to facilitate relaxation and the free energy exchange. Whoever takes the passive role should lie down (face up or down, depending on the type of massage) and breathe deeply and in a coordinated fashion with their partner. The partner who assumes an active role must be sitting. This way, the giver is above its partner and can move their hands freely and without stress.

The Four Basic Positions of the Hands

The four positions of the hands during the massage are a fundamental part of successfully providing the massage. Each of these positions entail different energy flows and, therefore, has different effects on the couple's body. It's essential to keep in mind that, whatever the position chosen for a certain stage of massage, fingers and hands should always be relaxed and move lightly and smoothly. The giver shouldn't lose sight of what's going on.

Bear in mind that this is not a kinesiological practice, but a series of massages intended to harmonize your bodies in a physical and spiritual fashion. This way it's possible to unlock areas of the body that are energetically obstructed–either partially or totally. In this way, it's possible to subsequently enjoy such erotic moment. Therefore, excessive pressure is not recommended. A soft touch is the best way to go. Think of this as a way of seducing and attracting energy rather than forcing it.

The four ways to place your hands are as follows:

1.   Percussion: The fists are closed without force and by alternating hands, the giver drops them repeatedly and rhythmically over the body area that they are taking care of. In such a way that it's possible to stimulate energy quickly.

2.   Handling with the extended hand: In this way, the hand is extended with the fingers stretched, from palm to massage, and a certain part of the body is covered. It can be done in a straight line, in a circular way, or through a combinatorial of both. This is the best way to boost energy throughout the body. However, this should be done more slowly and by placing less pressure in comparison with the last hand position.

3.   Finger manipulation: In this position, the fingertip of the middle and first fingers should be utilized. The other fingers are not unused, but it can entail a certain pain risk for the giver due to its difficulty. As in the previous mode, it has the capacity of mobilizing energy. However, it does so in an extremely subtle way.

4.   Stretching: It is mainly used to traverse the sides of the body, and it consists of operating with the hands as tweezers. The thumb and the upper palm should then be in contact with the lower side of the partner's body. It has a similar effect as with massage.

The Order of the Massages

During the initial phase, it is more convenient to start working on the back, which is why this stage is usually known as the dorsal phase. The reasoning of starting in this body part is that's less threatening for the one who receives the massage. In this way, it is easier to access and transfer energy. Furthermore, it helps to stimulate sexual energy.

The second stage focuses on the frontal part of the body. This way, it results more stimulating, both for the one who's giving the massage and as well as for one who's receiving it. This step is called the frontal stage. The session should conclude with a brief massage that focuses on the face. The objective of this stage is to stabilize the body's energy and prepare the receiver to return to a normal state of consciousness.

Essential Oils

Incorporating oils into the massage greatly facilitates the task for the partner who performs it and increases the pleasure of the receiver. What is more, there are some essential oils that have aphrodisiac properties when they are used. Of course, the degree of erotic stimulation increases when using them. Fragrances, which are the most recommended in this regard are cinnamon, ylang-ylang, jasmine cedar, sandalwood, vanilla and patchouli.

For making the most of the massage, it is recommended to:

- Take a warm and comforting bath beforehand. A normal bath can work perfectly for this purpose. The best option, though, is undoubtedly an immersion bath that lasts at least twenty minutes. For this, you can add some essential oils to the bathtub—such as sandalwood, lavender, rose, etc.

- Warm your hands before starting. This is of great importance for the partner who's having an active role during the massage—i.e. the giver. To do this, you can wash your hands by rubbing your palms against each other until they get to the right temperature.

- Always have clean and conveniently cut nails.

- Curate the atmosphere of the place where the massage

is going to performed—so that's pleasant for both the receiver and the giver.

- Be certain that the room is properly heated to avoid unpleasant and harmful effects of cold.

Massages for the Dorsal Stage

In the following lines, there are some important aspects of stimulating the back portion of the body. The minimum duration of each massage should be at least five minutes. Extending that time will deepen the benefits. Nevertheless, benefits can be noticed if the massage is performed for a shorter period.

Stimulation of the back and chest
This massage relaxes the upper back and chest area and harmonizes the fourth chakra.

- Close your fists without stressing them.

- Place them suspended in the air above the area of the shoulder blades

- Drop them alternately on the back in a slow and regular fashion.

- Toward the end of the massage, let the rhythm to slow

down gradually until finishing it.

Shoulder massage

The following practice has the potential of preventing and countering diseases. Furthermore, it also produces a notable increase of energy and desire.

- Place the palms on each shoulder blade with the fingers pointing toward the sacrum.

- Push down slowly and firmly, using the extended hand technique and following a path along both sides of the column.

- Return by performing friction in the column, using the thumbs of both hands.

Column shaking

The technique explained here is called such because it causes a certain "shaking" in the body for the one who receives the massage. However, it eliminates postural tensions and facilitates the free flow of energy, with the consequent benefit that this potentiates sexuality.

- Place the fingertips of both hands at the base of the seventh cervical vertebra (the protruding neck bone).

- Move your fingers back and forth at a rapid pace.

- Go down with that same movement until you reach the sacrum.

Column scaling

This massage allows for the receiver to relax and works some of the muscles around the back.

- Place the left hand on the sacrum with the fingers in front of it.

- Put the right hand in front of the left, also with the fingers facing toward the head.

- Exert slight pressure with the left hand without moving it.

- Press lightly with the right hand and (keeping that pressure) start an ascending path through each vertebra, using the manipulation with the extended hand until the fingers arrive at the back portion of the head.

Sacral Desobstruction

The practice here described has the potential of decreasing sciatic and lumbar pains, as well as preventing and countering vaginismus and impotence.

- Place your hands one of each side of the sacrum with

your fingers pointing toward the head.

- Push the center line of the sacrum with your thumbs, in a diagonal movement that goes from the bottom up and inside out.

Work on the legs

It allows to release sexual inhibitions and (therefore) eliminate resistance to new experiences, both emotional and sexual ones.

- Place your hands on the ankles with the palms on the inside portion.

- Move up slowly until you reach the groin.

- Move down through the outer part until you return to the ankles.

Massages for the Frontal Stage

In the same way as with the dorsal stage, here are some ideas to go through the frontal area of the body. As mentioned before, the minimum duration of each of the massages detailed here should be five minutes.

Resting Position

This massage increases confidence within the couple and facilitates energy transfer for the one who's receiving the massage. The main way to do so is to place the hands and move them throughout the fourth chakra. This way it's possible to increase the desire of emotional unity.

- Place the palm of the left hand vertically in the middle portion of the chest with the fingers facing the pubic area.

- Apply a very light pressure.

- Coordinate your respiratory rhythm with your partner.

Pectoral Massages

These massage help overcome inhibitions and work on energetic blockages that could affect full enjoyment. What is more, it also improves respiratory problems and release chest tension.

- Place your fists in a closed way (without stressing them) on the center part of the sternum, within the central pectoral zone.

- Exert a very light pressure and (once done) perform circular and regular movements. Do so first clockwise and then in the opposite direction.

Position for the Solar Plexus

This technique, as the name implies, aims to revitalize the solar plexus. As a result, it relaxes the diaphragm and it gives a greater sense of self-confidence to the receiver. Likewise, when acting on the solar plexus, it does the same with Manipura – the third chakra.

- Rest the palm of the left hand on the upper part of the abdomen, below the sternum, with the fingers pointing downwards.

- Exert a very soft and direct the hand toward the pubic bone, without moving it. Return to the starting position.

Lower Abdomen Massage

This massage produces a feeling of confidence and comfort. At the same time, it subtly stimulates sexual energy.

- Rest the palm of the left hand on the abdomen lower, so that the fingers touch the upper end of the pubic bone.

- Let the heat and energy of the palms flow to your partner's body.

Arm Massage

The following massage helps to lighten tensions and allows the receiver to let themselves go and enjoy the moment.

- Take your partner's hand, holding it gently but firmly by the wrist.

- Place your free hand on your partner's palm and, from there, slowly start your way up until you reach the armpit—always on the inner side of the arm.

- Upon reaching the armpit, go over the shoulder and (from there) go slowly through the outer side of the arm until reaching the knuckles.

- Do the same on the other arm.

Energy Shift

This powerful massage has the capacity of collecting and transport body energy to the genital area.

- Place your palms in the central part of the sternum.

- Slowly, slide them toward the pubic bone using the finger tips to direct the hands.

- Upon reaching the pubic bone, separate the hands and travel throughout the bones of the hips.

- From there, slowly climb up the sides to the armpits.

- Return to the center of the sternum.

Frontal Leg Massage

This massage can potentially make energy blocks disappear and noticeably increase the flow of general vitality.

- Place one of the palms on the inside of the ankle.

- Move up slowly until you reach the upper portion of the thighs.

- Move down through the outer side of the leg until you return to the ankles.

Massages for the Final Stage

As mentioned before, an erotic massage session must conclude with the face area. This has the aim of having the massage receiver to finish completely harmoniously and in total connection with you–after experiencing the multiple energy changes, as a direct result of the massages.

The following massages should be done sitting behind the head of the receiver.

Ears

Take the earlobes with the thumb and forefinger and massage them in a circular way. Then, grab the entire of the ear with your whole hand. Put pressure slightly and perform a movement from top to bottom and in reverse direction.

Forehead

Rest your fingers on the sides of the head and place your thumbs in the center of the forehead, just above the eyebrows. Exert a slight pressure and slowly direct the thumbs toward the temples.

Cheeks

Place your thumbs in the center of the forehead and the indexes to both sides of the nose. Apply a constant and moderate pressure while sliding the fingers out.

Chin

Draw a downline with your thumbs from the outer part of the lips to the chin.

Sexual Acupressure

Acupressure is the technique that consists in pressing with fingers on precise points to obtain certain effects. The cause of this is that the pressure exercised acts on energy regulations and, consequently, it eradicates the tensions generated by an excess of energy.

The effects produced by practicing acupressure can be very diverse–such as having therapeutic or just relaxing outcomes. However, this chapter focuses on the sexual outcome of acupressure. The latter means that it allows to increase the flow and the power of Kundalini energy. Therefore, this technique enhances arousal sexual and physical abilities required for erotic purposes.

In terms of sexuality, acupressure can be quite useful to establish constructive communication between you and your partner. This technique is not to stimulate directly the erogenous zones, but it facilitates the process of creating an atmosphere in which exercising simple and small point pressures leads to generate an energy vibration. In such way, waves start to trigger erotic stimulation.

The erotic points of acupressure are the following:

1.   Two symmetrical points on the sides of the nose.

2.   The area between the bottom of the junction of nasal holes and the central portion of the upper lip.

3.   Between the pubis and the belly button, just about three inches of the latter.

4.   Four different points on the horizontal line in the area above the pubis.

5.   A finger above the interior area.

6.   The tip of the second toe of the left foot.

7.   Between the third and fourth lumbar vertebra, one centimeter on top of the buttocks.

8.   One centimeter above the previous point.

9.   The vertical line of points on the sacrum.

10. The V line that brings together the points on the buttocks.

Chapter 4: Mind-blowing Techniques of Tantric sex

This chapter explains two types of experiences that can be carried out by regular practitioners of tantric sex. Likewise, these are ideal for those who are already accustomed to performing the maithuna. Therefore, they are able to put charges into play with extraordinary energy. These are rituals dedicated to the Gods. Such practices are known in the West as "group sex."

In the first case, the energy load put into play is truly exceptional since in the ceremonies that are detailed here also summons the explicit invocation of one or more divinities-although all forms of maithuna are a way that a man and a woman summon their inner gods.

In the second case, during collective miathunas it's essential to bear in mind that they are not simply orgies as we might understand in the West. They are, though, energetic and spiritual ceremonies that utilizes sex as a path toward transcendence and enlightenment.

Shiva Shakty Ritual

1. This ceremony aims to unify the consciousness, the connection to what's happening in this precise moment with eternity. Furthermore, it helps to overcome the boundaries of ego, time and space to access a higher plane.

2. Bathe before starting the rite. The bath must be taken individually so that physical contact happens only during the beginning of the actual ritual.

3. The man must wear yellow clothes preferably and, thus, representing the day, the sun and the masculine energy. The woman should be in black to symbolize the night, the moon, and the feminine energy.

4. It is preferable that the room for the ceremony has a floor covered with carpets, cushions, and pillows. Furthermore, it must allow freedom of movement. It is also quite essential that there is a proper musical background. In addition, all inspiring decorations are welcome such as flowers, candles, incense, etc.

5. Only once you've completed all of what was described before, create a circle in the room. This can be done either in a mental or physical way–through flower petals, a rope, or drawing the circle with chalk.

6. Women and men stand in the center of the circle. Afterward, the women will place the palms of their hands on the middle of the chest and, looking at his partner in the eyes, he will recite: "I am the power of the feminine and the principle of life. I am Shakty. I am the girl, the woman, the companion, the mother, the wise, the magician, and the old woman. I receive you, Shiva, Man, God."

7. In the same position, the man will say: "I am Shiva, power of the masculine, the light and spiritual impulse. I am the boy, the man, the partner, the father, the wise, the magician, and the patriarch. I receive you, Shakty, woman, Goddess."

8. Then, both will say at the same time: "I offer you my dance." Afterward, you will begin to move your body freely within the circle. Be sure to always breathe slowly and deeply, in such a way that allows the dance to mobilize the energy within your bodies.

9. As the body heat increases, you can start taking off your clothes–being careful that this always happens within the circle. In this way, you're offering your nudity to your partner in a physical and emotional sense.

10. Continue dancing naked without touching each other for about 15 minutes and then sit face to face. Keep your

back straight and your legs crossed. Stare into each other's eyes with love and devotion.

11. Hold hands. Approximate your noses without touching each other and inhale the air that the other exhales, for not less than 15 minutes. This will allow the aura to be energetically fed back after the fatigue, which might have been caused due to dancing.

12. At the end of the breathing stage, you'll begin to play throughout your bodies. Leave the genital until the very end.

13. After several minutes of caresses, feel how the Kundalini energy has been already activated. The man will sit on the floor and the woman will climb on him so as to be penetrated.

14. In this position, you'll perform smooth and delicate movements. It's crucial that you pay proper attention on breathing, making it as deep and as conscious as possible. It is important to keep in mind that this isn't just another sexual encounter. This is a special ritual. Due to that reason, the more slow and deep breathing you perform, the chances decrease for the man to ejaculate before the woman reaches an orgasm. Furthermore, you'll both feel an ascension of energy.

15. You and your partner will be able to mentally visualize

Kundalini energy like a snake that unfolds through the ritual. In this way, the chakras are stimulated deeply.

16. Once both of you've reached an orgasmic state, you'll stop on a smooth fashion until the ritual is over.

Kali Goddess Ritual

Kali is the passionate sexual initiator and the goddess who owns a supreme creative and destructive power. She does not know fear and is the one who transforms consciousness. The following ritual allows you to connect with anyone. What is more, the Kali Goddess Ritual helps to break the boundaries of the ego. Therefore, you'll be able to access a higher level of consciousness due to sensuality.

1. During one night, undress and draw a ritual circle (with petals, chalk, etc.) and start the ceremony by proclaiming the following sentence: "Kali, female spirit full of courage and passion, initiator Goddess of mysteries, bridge that unites the mundane and the transcendent, divinity capable of granting liberation through sex and wisdom: hold me in your arms. And with it, destroy my weaknesses and temper my spirit. Undress me from the inside so that I can see the light."

2. Begin to dance erotically while feeling the atmosphere

of the moment. At this point, you should attempt to connect through the movements with the energy of the Kali goddess. Visualize her as a beautiful woman with long black hair, four arms, a beautifully curved body. She has very intense eyes and a long tongue which is held out and evoking the fire of sexual passion.

3. At the middle of the dance, start repeating the mantra of Kali (Om kang kalika namah) for a minimum of 15 minutes. This was her presence and energy of Kali become more powerful and palpable.

4. When you've considered that they you've recited the mantra enough times, move to a more meditative space. The man will close his eyes and visualize the mandala (mystical diagram) corresponding to the honored goddess, which are a series of five equilateral triangles inserted one inside the other and placed on a lotus flower with eight petals. At the center of it all, there's a small point that symbolizes the stability of consciousness.

5. Once connected internally with Kali's mandala, the woman will support her body on her buttocks and will take the tip of her feet with each hand. She'll then lift them until he is in balance. The man will meditate on her naked yoni and will kiss her and drink from her energetic fluids.

6. The man will lie on his back, relaxing his body, and the woman, incarnating Kali will stand on top of him.

7. The male will touch the erogenous zones of his partner's body.

8. When they feel that desire is truly powerful, the woman will stick out her tongue as much as possible. Afterward, she'll introduce the lingam in her wet yoni. Then they will perform the maithuna. Stay in this position so as to allow the undulating movements of the body of the goddess Kali embodied in the woman.

9. With the sexual organs together, men and women will repeat the mantra of Kali again every time they're exhalating. This will allow you to completely loosen up your individual egos and reach a sexual and spiritual climax. After that, you to then stay in a state of complete silence, bliss and meditative ecstasy.

10. Finish the ritual by thanking Kali.

Collective Maithunas

Part of the tantric tradition argues that emotions can be exalted if there's the presence of a third party or somebody else participating in a form of collective sexual rituals. Tantra affirms that sex between three or more people if it's practiced for a spiritual sake. The most common forms of collective maithunas are the sexual encounters that are performed with two women and one man. The woman has an eminently receptive nature. Furthermore, because among most of them there is a feeling of brotherly solidarity, eroticism and sensuality, which consequently generates attraction and unity. These collective sex encounters are called by Tantra "Secret Games." Its importance is such that it was a common practice among Indian emperors and kings.

The sacred tantric book of Chandamaharosana describes group sex in the following way: "A woman from the moon is enjoyed by another one similar to her. The third person differs from the other two and must balance her strength. When enjoyed together, they all free themselves from decay and of death. He stimulates them both. They excite each other and they combine with him. The two moons are always full of nectar and the sun burns without being consumed." For the purpose of unity for three to occur, self-interest and strong emotions should disappear. Otherwise, these experiences would become something mundane, far from the tantric goal of transcendence.

Another sexual practice of a collective nature is the so-called Ritual of the Five Senses. This ritual consists of the union of a man with five different women, in which each of them represents a different sense. This way, the five senses are stimulated to obtain spiritual liberation.

Chakra Puja Ritual

Chakra Puja means "circular cult" and is performed with eight couples (man-woman). Each of them makes up a circle and have their own encounters. The ritual consists of stopping before reaching an orgasm. Afterward, the next couple begins to have sex and stops before the climax. They do the same, and they go on. This way, a very powerful accumulation of energy is created. This particular ritual allows participants to reach a state of ecstasy besides erotic enjoyment.

Yoguini Chakra Ritual

In the past, this rite was practiced by tantric monarchs to procreate enlighten children. This ritual is practiced between a man and an odd number of women—e.g. three, five, or seven of them. The man and his partner are placed in the center while surrounded by the remaining women. Alternatively, each woman will have a short encounter with the man. The man would not spread his semen to the other women. He'd absorb the women's energy to finally grant it to his partner.

Bhairavi Chakra Ritual

A woman stands naked in the center of a circle, representing the goddess Kali. The couples participating in the rite offer her flowers, fruits, and drinks. After doing so, they make up a circle and then they start performing the maithuna.

Group Sex in the Kama Sutra

According to the Kama Sutra, when a man enjoys two women at the same time, he should love them equally. When a man performs maithuna at the same time with several women, this union is called "the pack of cows." There are several types of unions and some of them are as following:

- The water union (which is also known as the elephant union) is a ritual only takes places in the water.

- The union of the pack of goats or the union of the pack of hinds, is called due to its similarity to the movements of this animal.

- In some cases, several young men practice maithuna with a woman who may be the partner of one of them. One holds her, while the other enjoys her. A third man over her mouth, a fourth caresses her navel. Each man alternates in each position.

Chapter 5: Mastering Tantric Sex

In Tantric sex, the atmosphere is key to have deep and meaningful encounters with your partner. The place and time of the encounters are of vital importance insofar as they can determine if the act will be successful. Mastering tantric sex can be achieved by taking care of the elements surrounding the happening. All these are preparational steps that are necessary and should be addressed beforehand.

In this chapter, we're going to further discuss the elements that need to be in check in order to enjoy a full tantric experience.

The foods of love

The foods, which are commonly known as "aphrodisiacs," have a reputation of awakening or stimulating the sexual appetite. The name of these foods comes from Aphrodite; the Greek goddess of love that emerged from the foam of the sea when the god Cronos killed and castrated his father Uranus. After it, Cronos threw Uranus' genitals and (subsequently) Aphrodite emerged from the sea.

There's a large number of foods that are capable of rising one's sexual arousal. Most aphrodisiacs usually work by stimulating some senses (sight, touch, smell, and hearing). Since ancient times, these numerous foods have helped people to raise their sexual arousals.

In the following lines you'll find a summarized guide of the foods have the most aphrodisiac effects. Basil

The use of this plant for erotic purposes is known by several cultures and has given rise to all kinds of myths and legends.

Summer Savory

This is type of grass which is native to the Caucasus, is normally used to dress meats and salads. Using on a daily basis is enough to enjoy of its aphrodisiac effects. Garlic

Its greatest quality is that it remarkably helps the body to stay healthy, which translates into an increase of vital energy and an increase in sexual performance. Its fame as an aphrodisiac food is also due to the warming effect it produces in the body when ingested.

Musk Mallow

It is a variety of mallow that is native to the East Indies. The infusions made with its leaves have a recognized aphrodisiac effect while the paste obtained from crushing its seeds is extremely effective in treating sexual impotence.

Celery

Like any food that acts on the urinal organs, celery has a moderate aphrodisiac effect. It also contains iron, magnesium, phosphorus and sulfur, which makes it exceptionally revitalizing.

Cinnamon

This is a popular aphrodisiac that was already used in ancient times as seasoning and in the form of massage oil. His original name was "Cacynnama," which meant "aromatic wood." It's effective and strong sexual stimulant, especially for women. It's usually used mainly to season desserts. However, you can also include it in soups, stews and salads or to add flavor to drinks.

Cardamom

An oriental plant of spicy taste and characteristic perfume, this spice has been considered as one of the most important condiments of India. It works perfectly to revitalize one's sexual arousal.

Chocolate

Chocolate is rich in antioxidants and has an exquisite taste. Chocolate is a magnificent aphrodisiac.

Curry

This is a flavoring mixture composed of different spices. While there is no "fixed formula," its mainly composed by ginger, nutmeg, pepper, turmeric, mustard, cardamom, paprika, cloves, cinnamon and anise. Of course, it combines all the stimulating properties of each of its components. Pomegranate

Pomegranate has been considered a symbol of fertility among the ancient Romans. It has a medium, but not negligible, aphrodisiac effect.

Fig

In many places in Asia it's considered a powerful aphrodisiac. It was also seen that way by ancient Greeks and Romans.

Royal jelly

As a great general and sexual stimulant, it has a recognized restorative action that increases sexual strength in both sexes.

Ginger

This is an extremely important aphrodisiac vegetable, which enjoys of a great reputation since ancient times — especially in India, China, and Japan. The sexually stimulating properties of this root were very also appreciated in France during the reign of Louis XV, where they're sold in the form of pills. Currently, you can get this root (fresh or dried) almost anywhere. However, you might find them easily as dietary and supplementary pills. With the root, you can make an infusion or add it to various foods (chutneys, stews, desserts, etc.)

Apple

A symbol of sexuality par excellence, it's also known as "the forbidden fruit." It has a mild aphrodisiac effect. Seafood

While the oyster is considered as an aphrodisiac seafood for many, other seafood (e.g. clams, shrimps or prawns) also have an excellent reputation in this regard. Mint

It is the first medicinal plant that began to be used as an aphrodisiac due to its effectiveness as a mild stimulant of the system nervous. It can be used to make an infusion, to decorate desserts, or to chew its leaves. Mint has the additional advantage that it refreshes and perfumes your breath — which is uncommon among other aphrodisiac foods. Honey

It's an efficient source of energy that is rich in minerals and vitamins. Its properties as a restorative for lovers are well known since ancient times. The purer the honey, the more effective it is as an aphrodisiac.

Nutmeg

Nutmeg has a sweet, soft, and seductive aroma. In India is used as aphrodisiac for women. Oysters

These are the undisputed start regarding all the aphrodisiac seafood. They are high in mineral content and can be cooked. However, their affect is greater if consumed raw. Avocado

This fruit is highly appreciated for its ability as a stimulant sexual, which is due to its high content of vitamins D and E — which provides great energy value. Its seed is claimed to improve virile potency. For this, it's convenient to soften the seed in milk before eating it.

Paprika

It has a high capsaicin content (which is present in many spicy aphrodisiac food). As other peppers, it's a strong sexual stimulant — although is less spicy than other peppers. Chili Pepper

This is one of many stimulating spices and its well known for its aphrodisiac effects. In particular, it has a powerful effect in the pelvic area.

Tomato

Tomato contains matadine that works to synthesize sexual hormones.

Ginseng root

This herbaceous plant has been used in East Asia as an aphrodisiac for a long time. For more than four millennia as it has a reputation for having extraordinary properties as a stimulant for men. According to ancient Hindu medicine books, ginseng endows young people and the elders of an incredible sexual force. It has a characteristic tuber root, whose appearance might be similar to the one of a human being. Its two best known varieties are Panax Ginseng (native of the East) and Panax quinquefolium, native to eastern North America.

Ginseng increases resistance to tiredness, fights the harmful effects of stress, stimulates the nervous central system, and improves brain activity — which has strong sexual effects. In addition to its beneficial effects regarding physical capabilities that come with the aphrodisiac effects, it's totally harmless and free of contraindications contrary to chemical stimulants. Its most common uses are to combat the sexual fatigue among lovers, frigidity of women, and male impotence. You can easily get it in specialty stores, and it's available in different forms. The best known presentation are capsules and tea bags. Ingest ginseng a half hour before having a sexual encounter. A good alternative is a well-loaded ginseng tea with ground pepper.

Alcoholic beverages

Alcoholic beverages have the power to ignite sexual arousal. However, this depends on how much you ingest. A little bit of a good drink has the capacity to relax the body and ward off inhibitions. But it will have the opposite effect if taken in excess. Alcohol can be an anaphrodisiac beverage whose most counterproductive effects will be that of paralyzing the sexual organs. The quality of alcohol is also very crucial. A high-quality drink taken in a moderate amount can be a true love tonic capable of dilating blood vessels and radiating heat through the skin, next to another series of more subtle effects.

Yohimbine

The bark of this tree, which is originally from Africa, constitutes an aphrodisiac that acts quite fast and is extremely effective. It is one of the most studied sexual potentiation drugs. Such tests have been run especially in animals. In rats it has been shown that it enhances sexual arousal. The effect on humans, however, has been much less studied. It's only known to help men in improving the quality of their erections. An infusion can easily be prepared by pouring half a liter of boiling water over fifteen grams of Yohimbine crust. The latter should be finely crumbled and then should be left to soak for a half hour. Bear in mind that you should not consume more than 30 drops of this liquid. If lemon juice is added (which will provide you vitamin C), the outcome will be even better. Likewise, consider that it should never be mixed with alcohol. Now that we have covered some of the most important foods to potentiate your sexual experiences, let's go through a quick but comprehensive list of recipes for you to cook.

Entrees
Crab Salad
4 endives
10 asparagus
1/2 package of arugula
4 crab legs
Olive oil

Salt and pepper

Place the endives at the bottom of the plate, the tips of the cooked asparagus and the arugula leaves. On that bottom, place the legs of the crab and season with the oil, salt and pepper.

Sweet and sour avocado salad

2 avocados

1 medium size tomato

1 tablespoon coriander

4 slices of bacon

1/2 onion

4 tablespoons vinegar

1 spoon of sugar

Cayenne pepper

Peel and cut the avocados into small cubes. Cut the tomatoes into a cube. Chop the cilantro and place all of these ingredients into a bowl. Put aside. Cook the bacon in a pan at medium heat until it is crunchy. Remove the bacon and, with its fat, sauté the sliced onion until it's transparent. Add the vinegar, sugar, and pepper and wait until it is boiling. Pour the hot dressing over the bowl and serve immediately, placing the bacon slices on top.

Shrimp salad

2 cups of cooked and peeled shrimp

1 cup of celery white

2 cups of watercress leaves

1 slice of pineapple

2 tablespoons of cream

2 tablespoons of natural yogurt

1 tablespoon of lemon juice

Salt and pepper

Place the shrimp, chopped celery, watercress leaves in a bowl. Cut the pineapple into small pieces. Dress with cream, yogurt, lemon, salt and pepper.

Cold Soup of Avocado, Cucumber, and Tomato

1 avocado

2 cups of broth

1/2 cup natural yogurt

1 tablespoon of lemon juice

1 large tomato

1 cucumber

2 tablespoons fried croutons

Salt and pepper

Place in a blender the following ingredients: avocado, broth, yogurt, lemon juice, salt and pepper. Blend until the mixture is homogeneous. Pour into a bowl. Add the tomato and the cucumber. Make sure that they're cut in small cubes. Serve cold with croutons of bread.

Main courses
Curried vegetables
1 and 1/2 cup of green beans
1 and 1/2 cup of broccoli
1 green pepper
1 onion
2 eggplants
2 cloves of garlic
1 cup of coconut milk
2 cups of water
1 teaspoon of chopped and fresh ginger
1 teaspoon of curry (preferably not a non-spicy one)
2 tablespoons of peanuts
Salt and pepper

Simmer the coconut milk for 15 minutes with the water. Afterward, add the curry, ginger and garlic, making sure that they're all finely chopped. Afterward, add the green beans, broccoli, chili pepper, onion and eggplants, which should be cut into small pieces. Let everything cook until the vegetables are ready. Add salt and pepper and serve with some peanuts in the middle.

Tortilla with caviar and pine nuts

5 eggs

2 tablespoons of caviar

4 tablespoons of cream

1 teaspoon of grated and fresh ginger

2 cloves of garlic

1 tablespoon of coriander

4 tablespoons of pine nuts

2 tablespoons of butter

A few drops of Tabasco sauce.

Salt and pepper

Beat the eggs and add the cream, the Tabasco sauce, the ginger, salt and pepper. Slowly add the caviar. Put aside when ready. In a pan, fry the whole garlic cloves in the butter. When they're golden brown, remove them from the stove. Add the finely chopped cilantro. Add the mixture that had been put aside and let it set over low heat.

Turn it over and cover until an omelet is formed. Serve it with escarole salad and black olives. You can also season it with olive oil, lemon juice, and salt.

Spiced Kebab

1 lb. of minced beef

10 fresh mint leaves

1/2 cup of chives

1 tablespoon of ground black pepper

1 teaspoon of cumin powder

1/2 teaspoon of cinnamon

Salt

Place all ingredients in a bowl. Make sure that the chives and the mint are finely chopped. Mix the ingredients very well. Form the kebabs, making sure that they're about 10 cm long and that they've the thickness of a big sausage. Roast on the grill after having add a little bit of oil. Serve with green apples and celery salad. Don't forget to season with olive oil, lemon juice, and salt.

Sauces

Guacamole

1 large avocado

1/2 tomato

Lemon Juice

1/2 onion

1 teaspoon of hot sauce

Salt and pepper

Peel the avocado and crush it with a fork until it looks like cream. Add the diced tomato, the onion (which has to be finely chopped), lemon juice, sauce, salt and pepper.

It can be served with both raw and cooked vegetables, as well as cold meats or with crackers.

Curry sauce

1/2 cup of chopped onion

4 tablespoons of butter

2 tablespoons of curry powder

2 tablespoons of cornstarch

1/2 liter of broth

1/2 cup of cream

1 tablespoon of lemon juice

Salt and pepper

Boil the broth and set aside. Melt the butter in a bowl. Sauté the onion and curry over low heat. Add the cornstarch and the broth. Boil and add the milk cream and lemon juice. Afterward, add the salt and pepper. You can use curry sauce to season white or red meats. Likewise, you can eat it with crackers.

Walnut sauce

2 tablespoons of chopped walnuts

2 tablespoons of olive oil

1 pot of natural yogurt

1 tablespoon of lemon juice

Salt and pepper

Drain the yogurt on a paper filter until the yogurt has a better consistency. Mix this with lemon juice and add the oil slowly. Add salt, pepper, and the chopped nuts. This is a great alternative to season salads and roasted vegetables.

Desserts

Pomegranate hearts

4 large pomegranates

1/2 cup whole sugar or honey

1 tablespoon agar-agar

4 tablespoons of cold water

Roll the grenades by hand, and knead to soften. Cut them in half and hit them gently to get all the berries from the inside. Blend the berries. Pour the juice over a small pan and add honey or sugar. Heat while stirring until everything is well dissolved. Add the agar-agar. Pour into two heart-shaped molds and cool until it's hard.

• Chocolate cream

6 bars of dark chocolate

3 eggs

3 tablespoons of cold water

2 tablespoons of sugar

1/2 cup of cream

Cookies

In a bowl, place the chocolate and cold water and melt in a water bath. Remove from the heat and add, the yolks one by one while beating them. Afterward, add the sugar. Let it cool and set aside.

In another bowl, beat the cream until it's firm and add the chocolate mix with smooth movements. In a third bowl, beat the egg whites until they are firm and carefully add a spoon of the chocolate mixture. Pour into a bowl and refrigerate until it's set.

Serve it with cookies.

Slow fire

17 oz of milk

1/2 cup of peeled and chopped almonds

1/2 cup of cream

2 egg yolks

1 cup of honey

1 teaspoon of cinnamon

1/2 tablespoon of cornstarch

Heat almost all of the honey and almonds over low heat and until it boils. Pour the honey with almonds next to the cream, the yolks, what remains of the honey and cinnamon in a blender. Mix everything until it softens. Dissolve the cornstarch in a little bit of cold milk. Afterward, add it to hot milk.

Pour the cornstarch milk and eggs over the mixture obtained and stir until is thick, creamy and uniform.

Drinks

Pomegranate cocktail

2 grenades

2 glasses of ice water

1/2 glass of lemon juice

Honey

Remove the skin and seeds of the pomegranates and place the pulp in a blender. Add water, lemon juice, and honey. Blend until a homogeneous mixture is obtained. Serve in tall glasses and garnish with a mint leaf.

Rosemary wine

6 cups of red wine

6 branches of fresh rosemary

1 orange peel

1 vanilla bean

1 tablespoon of ground cinnamon

1 cup of sugar

Pour the wine into a non-metallic container and add the rosemary, the orange peel, vanilla, and cinnamon. Cover and let the mix to set for a period of 10 days. After that time, add the sugar and mix well until is dissolved. Strain the liquid, bottle, and cover with corks.

Cardamom coffee

Place a cardamom berry in a cup of coffee. Pour the coffee and let it set for a few seconds. Remove the berry and serve as usual

Vitamins and Nutrients That Can Improve Your Sexual Life

In addition to being necessary for health, vitamins play an essential role regarding sexual functions. Vitamins act on the endocrine glands, which in turn control the reproductive system.

Vitamin A feeds the mucous membranes that lubricate the sexual organs. Such vitamin can be found in mustard, fatty fish (salmon, herring), squash, spinach, kale and melon.

Vitamin B produces hormones and supplies them to the pituitary gland that stimulates the sex glands and is indispensable for hormonal balance. It can be found in fish, oats, milk, brewer's yeast and soy.

Vitamin D (which stimulates the sexual drive) can be obtained sunbathing. However, it can be found in cod liver oil.

Vitamin E is the most important in regard to sexuality, since it prevents sterility and is essential for effective functioning of all other vitamins. Some good sources of this vitamins are carrot, eggs, celery, parsley, whole wheat flour, and milk

Among the most important aphrodisiac mineral nutrients are iron and copper. These can be obtained from beets, spinach, lentils, red meat, oysters, and almost all legumes. Iodine is found in fish and shellfish, as well as in algae and iodized salt. Finally, phosphorus can be found in cheese, milk, eggs, potatoes and cauliflower.

Food for maithuna

Given that maithuna is a prolonged and hard ritual that can last several hours, it requires large amounts of energy. Due to that reason, it's recommendable to have some foods at hand during the encounter including some of the dishes that were mentioned before.

Another good option in this regard is to have some fresh fruits. As for drinks, water and fruit juices are excellent, as well as alcoholic beverages such as champagne or wine. Be mindful of not abusing of them.

Furthermore, a great option to increase passion between lovers is to play sexual games with food. Some examples are the following:

- Spread whipping cream on different parts of the body, then lick and eat it.

- Place a small fruit (e.g. a grape or cherry) or a small piece of some larger fruit at the entrance of the vagina and eat it.

- Spread the penis with some jam or honey for oral sex.

- Spill honey on the buttocks and eat it.

The Importance of Pheromones

Pheromones are natural chemical aphrodisiacs. They are expelled by our bodies through secretions, which are produced by the skin and the mucous membranes. Our brains catch them through smell or taste, acting as a sexual signal. Due to this reason, it's useful to take care of our hygiene on a daily basis. The smell of genitals and other parts of the body can act as the most powerful of all aphrodisiacs.

Sometimes for the sake of smelling good, we make excessive use of deodorants. However, we tend to forget the effects of these substances in our bodies. Don't forget that natural methods to smelling well can help greatly to attract the attention of the opposite sex.

Some recommendations for segregating pheromones are the following:

- Do not take away the fresh sweat from your body. In general, bad smells appears only several hours after having transpired.

- Do not overuse deodorants. If you sweat a lot, I recommend you to use an odorless antiperspirant.

- Keep in mind that frequent sexual intercourse and regular oral sex increases naturally the productions of pheromones.

- There are commercial pheromones that have been produced in the lab. These can be bought in specialized stores. They often can be found as sprays and are totally odorless.

The place of maithuna

It shouldn't be surprising to assume that maithuna can be performed almost anywhere. However, the atmosphere of the place must also be prepared in several ways to harmonize fully with the sacred character of the ritual. All elements should be put in place to make the experience enjoyable and fulfilling. Therefore, it is essential to take into account the following considerations prior to maithuna.

The hygiene of the Site

It is extremely important that the chosen site, whatever it is, is neatly cleaned. In this way, the lovers have total freedom of movement and are not afraid of getting out of bed without getting their bodies dirty. Be sure to aromatize the space. The aromas in the place where this sacred will take place are extremely important. Be mindful that they constitute a central stimulus during the act.

While having a clean place is key, there's more that can be done in this sense. Aromatic candles have (in addition to a pleasant smells) the additional advantage of illuminating the environment in a particularly sensual way. Sensual incenses furthermore increase a sexual environment, preferably those with aphrodisiac fragrances such as sandalwood or rose. Some other good aromatic options are the following:

- Basil: its aphrodisiac powers are widely known in various cultures—as we mentioned before. This is a plant that can be placed in the place where the maithuna will take place or put a few drops in a nearby incense burner. Of course, use caution when burning any oil or incense.

- Artemis: when burning it flowers and leaves over coal unleash incredible effects to those who are reached by the smoke of this incense.

- Wormwood: it's recommended to burn its dried flowers; whose powerful aphrodisiac perfume is one of the most efficient ones.

- Coriander: the seeds of this plant can be crushed and mixed with musk and saffron, to get a powerful incense effect.

- Elecampane: when its leaves and stem are crushed and mixed then with a small amount of gray amber, they result in a paste with aphrodisiac effects when is burned.

- Lily: the stimulating properties of this plant are varied, and they can be obtained in different ways. One of them is to burn its dried flowers in the room where maithuna is to happen, guaranteeing this way a pleasant encounter.

It is worth mentioning again, that when using any type of burner for oils and incense, be sure to check from time to time to ensure that you don't start a fire. When deeply into tantric sex, it can remove you from your surroundings. Preferably, you'll use a burner that won't allow hot ashes to escape, and you'll put it in a place where it can't be knocked over. Be careful if you have pets to keep it away from them so that they don't accidentally tip it over. If it is possible to keep it in the same room that you are in, you should do so. Also, follow the same advice when burning candles. You can also opt for battery operated candles. Some are very realistic and flicker like a real candle, providing the same erotic effect.

Lights

Lovers must decide what kind of lighting to shelter their maithuna. In general, dim lighting is often the best option for this purpose. However, that depends deeply on what you enjoy the most. You can opt for a full lighting that allows to visualize every little detail of your partner's body. Conversely, you can choose total darkness to set aside the view and give a greater role to the remaining senses (smell, touch, taste, and hearing).

As said before, dim lighting is usually the most appropriate option. There are different modes of using it. The most common one is to use candles as discussed above. These should of different sizes and must be set in different places. Another alternative is to have one or several bulbs of different color—such as red, green, or orange. This way it's possible to obtain a special atmosphere. You can also cover a white bulb with some color to reproduce the latter suggestion.

Additionally, dark light is another great option when it comes to curate a special atmosphere.

Take Care of the Ear

The sense of hearing should not be forgotten at the time of prepare for maithuna. From a pure tantric perspective, the best way to produce an excellent atmosphere is by hearing music that can help you to relax. Some might be satisfied with Oriental sounds, which can be played on the background. If this isn't within your music likes, you can always switch to something that is more pleasant for you. Have in mind that for this to work, it should make you and your partner feel comfortable.

In all cases, it's important that the volume isn't too loud to cover the sounds produced by you. Nevertheless, another fine option is to have your background silent. This way the only music that sounds is the couple's intense and sound breathing along with the moans of pleasure and words of love.

Temperature

The temperature of the place where the maithuna will take place is a fundamental point to consider. If it's too warm, it will it will produce excess sweat. Therefore, you'll need to replenish fluids and constantly drink water, which can disrupt the experience. On the contrary, if the atmosphere is freezing, the lovers will be more concerned with being well covered. This will divert your attention, in addition to that fact that covered bodies do not move as freely as those that are naked. Therefore, it must be ensured that the temperature is comfortable.

Body hygiene: The Couple's Bathroom

Body hygiene and perfumes are a fundamental point when it comes to unify the bodies of the lovers. Therefore, an essential step for maithuna is taken in the bathroom. It's essential that before maithuna starts, the lovers take a bath to purify the body, as well as to get rid of dirt and bad odors. Of course, it can be done individually. However, doing it as a couple adds pleasant sensations by adding the possibility of performing erotic games inside the bathtub, and it can even initiate intercourse.

Taking a bath together can bring a new dimension to the relationship and help to discover and explore your bodies. In the case of using a bathtub, it's ideal to use some bath oil, since it allows a better sliding of the lovers' hands on each other's body. Once the bath is over, the skin should be silky and hydrated. This makes it more attractive when touching. Foams and bath salts are also an interesting complement, but do not bring such erotic benefits as oils.

If taking a common shower, glycerin soap is usually the more convenient option. Similar to bath oils, this soap lubricates the skin and makes erotic games easier. The best essences for the bath are those that have aphrodisiac effects like ylang-ylang, musk, rose, etc.

After the bath, you can also spray your body with some perfume, cologne or fragrances that are similar to those used for the bath. Try not to mix different aromas.

Tantric Dance

Daily tensions cause large energy blockages as well as fatigue and stress. Tantric dances allow you to release those energies that are stuck in a negative pole. Therefore, they can open our erotic awareness. Tantra uses dance as a means to energize the bodies. This causes a purification and a catharsis of the emotional, bodily, and erotic energies.

The moments to perform tantric dances are also crucial. Basically, there are two options. They can be done at any time, which it will always be beneficial in terms of strengthening the union of the couple and to keep a high level of Kundalini energy. The other alternative is to dance just before maithuna. This can be some kind of foreplay since it increases the levels of sexual arousal.

You should be aware that there are some tantric principles for dancing and are the following:

Disconnect the mind

Our mind is usually the origin of many of the things that stress us. When dancing tantrically, it is best to leave the command to the body and allow it to determine what and how things should be done.

Lose all areas of the body, especially the area of the pelvis

People with sexual blockages and inhibitions usually experience marked difficulties when moving the pelvis. In those cases, they should put special effort into doing so. Although this isn't a perfect approach, releasing the energy of this area through movement is extremely beneficial in terms of positive consequences for our sexual life. Breathe consciously

Air is energy that enters the body. When performing tantric dances, you should always be aware of how you are breathing. More specifically, that you're performing deep breathings. Make of this the purpose of dancing. Tantric dancing is not about moving arms and feet to the beat of the music. The whole body must be engaged in the movement: the neck, torso, pelvis, etc. Make sure that the way to breath helps to properly articulate your movements. Perceive the Kundalini energy

Shortly after starting to dance, you'll begin to feel a kind of fire in the pelvic area. That is the Kundalini energy that it's awakening. It will be necessary to become aware of it and raise it through the remaining chakras. During a tantric dance, shame, control and repressions should be put aside. This has the purpose of triggering the release of new and high sensations and emotions. When dancing, it is possible to break inner barriers to set aside the mind and fully experience the moment. You'll fully perceive the moment and place where the dance is happening.

Be always aware of the purposes of the dances

The objectives of tantric dances are to perceive your couple in different way and raise the Kundalini energy. Perform it together with your partner for 30 to 45 minutes. The ideal way is to do it naked, but it can also be carried out with light and comfortable clothing. As for music, whatever the couple likes can work. Although, soft music is best.

Chapter 6: Foreplay, Fellatio, and Cunnilingus in Tantric

Caresses

Writing about caresses could take thousands and thousands of pages. The many ways of affectionately and sensually touching another person are virtually unlimited. Not only in terms of how to perform them (e.g. fingertips, with the palm, with the back, gently, pinch-shaped, etc.), but also regarding the body part that is been caressed — i.e. the erogenous zones for the most part. Therefore, the intention of this section of the book is to provide summarized information. Bear in mind that a large portion of tantric doctrines are devoted to the importance of caresses in loving relationship.

Eastern Style Caresses

The caresses, both male and female, are a very important factor in the development of desire and sensations. Erotic oriental caresses are based on the combination of two different techniques: static pressures and dynamic pressure.

- Static pressures consist of putting pressure on a certain area of the lover's body, without performing movements of no type. Although for many of us this can be somewhat strange, the truth is that this has a high potential for erogenous. In women, these pressures must be carried out (in the first moment) on the hands, the ears, the nape, the abdomen, the waist and the inner thighs

Pressures on the breasts and genital are to be performed in more advanced phases. Once there, it should be exercised first on the testicles and then on the lingam, ascending from the base to the glans.

- Dynamic pressure is applied in the same areas and in the same order, but in this mode neither fingers nor hands will stop moving around the lover's body.

It's quite fundamental that during the first moments of maithuna, the two lovers touch each other's palms of their hands. This should be done just after they have been rubbed carefully and vigorously for approximately one minute. By placing these two poles on the couple's body, which was energized by friction, a powerful exchange of bioenergy happens if the hands of both are intertwined. This exchange of energy flow not only corresponds to an increase in general vigor that favors sexual activity, but also an exchange of sensibilities. It also facilitates the elimination of negative thoughts and blockages.

Beyond the initial moment of the maithuna ceremony, the contact with the palms of the hands can be redone in any moment and is very useful during penetration, whatever position is been performed.

Caresses on the Genitals

Stimulation in the lingam and the yoni should be carried out in progressive way. Woman's manipulation of male genitals can be done more or less freely, with the condition of not causing premature ejaculation. Stimulations in women, in change, must be done in a more delicate way.

Caress the Lingam

As we it was mentioned before, the manipulation of the male genitals allows a "freer" practice than those of its female counterpart. While the possible ways of caressing it will depend on the imagination of the lover in question, there a series of basic movements that can serve as a guide:

- Take the lingam firmly with your whole hand, surrounding it and make smooth upward and downward movements.

- Perform smooth circular movements in the glans. Due to the high sensitivity of this body part, it's always good to lubricate your fingers with saliva before doing this.

- Gently traverse the fingertip with one or two fingers, from beginning of the glans and vice versa.

- Touch the scrotum gently.

Cherish the Yoni

It is advisable not to directly stimulate the feminine genital area, but first caress the peripheral areas. Then progressively focus on the key areas (labia majora and minors and, especially, the clitoris). With great delicacy, the man you should excite the contour of the vulva with his fingertips. Generate some friction with pubic hair or those that cover the labia majora. The friction in these hairs and subsequent contact will produce a static electricity charge that will favor eroticization.

Gently, the male will stimulate the labia majora by friction as well as small and repeated pinches. Afterward, he should perform the same process with the labia minora. The labia majora are usually closed, resting on the female genital tract while protecting it. When the woman is excited, these lips unfold and extend toward the area of the crotch, which opens the internal genital parts. In this way, it leaves the labia minora and its intimate and sensitive structures visible.

Also, the labia minora are usually closed and with sexual arousal increases its volume. Then the man can make circular moves around the clitoris, which are increasingly close.

Five Steps of Supreme Pleasure

The caressing session described before has an aim to break down inhibitions and to be sexually stimulating. This will increase mutual desire and reach a deferred climax. In general, Western couples (and especially men) tend to penetrate soon after starting with foreplay, which often causes the woman to start intercourse without being sufficiently excited. This makes it difficult, and sometimes even directly impossible to reach a climax.

In the following lines, you'll find how to perform caresses during different stages. Be mindful that it's crucial to start several hours before starting a sexual encounter. First stage

- Undress and put yourself in a comfortable place that allows freedom of movement (bed, mattress, on the floor, etc.).

- Caress each other with gentle circular movements throughout the body, except for the breasts and genitals.

- Kiss in the area of the face and neck (including the mouth) but without going further down.

- You can freely change position during this phase.

- A minimum duration of one hour is recommended for

this stage.

Second stage
- Lie in the spoon position (on the side, woman and man looking at the same point so that man can hug to his partner behind).

- Enjoy the proximity of the bodies, but without starting to have intercourse. If this posture becomes too tempting, stand in front of each other. It can also be accompanied by kisses in the neck area. The minimum recommended duration for this is a half hour.

Third stage
- In this third stage, you go on to the caresses in the breasts and the genitals as the kisses continue.

- Caressing the genitals (especially the female ones) should consist of very soft friction.

- It is recommended that this phase does not last less than a half hour.

Fourth stage
- In this last phase, caresses the genitals in such a way that covers the entire length of the lingam or the elevation of the vulva, the clitoris, and eventually, the entrance of the vagina.

- It is very possible (although not unexpectable) that one

or both of you orgasm after this.

Caresses of the Female G point

To stimulate the G-spot, you should rest your finger gently and in an soft manner over this part, which is located in the internal wall of the vagina, just about two inches from the vaginal cavity. Stimulate it by modifying the rhythm and paying attention to your partner's reaction. This type of caress requires a lot of tact, since the man can speed up or slow down, increase or decrease the pressure and, thereby, vary the degree of excitement of his partner.

It is recommended to perform this type of touch when the hands are completely clean, and nails are well cut and clean. Some lubricant on the finger can make this move smoother. The sensations obtained will be of less intensity than those of clitoral orgasm but will allow a faster and greater climax after a number of repetitions. An orgasm can also occur simultaneously with the stimulation of the clitoris and other erogenous zones.

Caresses of the Male G Point

There are two ways to caress and stimulate this point in the man. The first one, which is the indirect one, is not as electrifying as the direct one. However, it can produce a very pleasant orgasm. For this, you just need to massage and gently press the perineum (the area that is between the testicles and the anus), with your fingers that will be stimulating the G-spot from the outside.

The second form, the direct one, is much more pleasant for the man, since it is inside the anus and implies action over point G more bluntly. To carry out this stimulation, the man should be very relaxed and put aside all homophobic prejudices, since it is perfectly normal to feel Pleasure in that area. To proceed with the stimulation, the woman must insert a well-lubricated finger into her lover's anus. Start by massaging the perineum and the edges of the anus to relax it and turn it on and, once the excitement is achieved, the penetration must be very soft, pressing slowly for him to get used to this new sensation Once you have arrived there, you will have discovered the point G of the man, which is five centimeters from the entrance of the anus, surrounded by fibrous tissues and soft muscles, which can experience small spasms, so if these occur, you should the penetration be suspended until they are reduced. When the G-spot is found, the area of massage should be massaged in a soft manner. With this massage, many men can experience an orgasm—although some may need additional stimulation in the penis.

Kisses

The kiss on the mouth is often the first expression of love in a partner. No matter what other kind of activities of erotic stimulation might be performed, kissing is and will continue to be one of the most stimulating erotic practices that a human being can experience.

There is an infinite variety of kisses: with closed or open lips, dry or wet, highly active or virtually immobile, vehement or otherwise tender, and so on. A good lover should know (and practice) the greatest possible number of kisses. You should also perform them in various areas of the body of your lover, especially in the erogenous zones. Although the first expression of love, as we referred to, is usually a kiss on the mouth, many other areas of the body can be stimulated by kissing them.

The First Kisses

As we said already, kissing on the mouth is usually the confirmation of the erotic attraction between two people and, therefore, constitutes the demonstration of love. Usually, that first kiss is followed by several of them. That interaction can be called the "first session" of kisses. This first session is of great importance because every first impression is transcendental. This is the reason why many of the relationships that could begin do not develop due to unpleasant first kisses.

From the tantric point of view, this series of kisses constitutes the first male and female energy exchange, and it is critical that is produced harmoniously and positively. This way is possible to stimulate the Kundalini energy of both partners. It's true that each couple is a unique and unrepeatable pair, thus each couple enjoys kissing in different ways. There's no infallible formula that can make a kiss work all of the time. However, there are certain patterns that can help and they are as follows:

- Start gently with closed lips or slightly open. Do not kiss with wet lips, open mouth, or using your tongue.

- Relax your lips but not to the point of not kissing in a firm and secure way.

- While kissing, gently touch your partner's back, shoulders and cheeks.

- Live that moment as if it was the first and last time, you're kissing each other. Enjoy it to the fullest.

- Then, proceed to kiss the remaining areas of the face.

- Return to the mouth. Finally, introduce slightly your tongue in the mouth of your partner. You can kiss deeper in a progressive manner.

- Alternate long kisses with short kisses.

Exercises to Kiss Better

Relaxation and flexibility in the area of the mouth and lips is something fundamental when practicing kissing. The relaxation of the tongue and lips allows to generate an exquisitely sensual feeling that is impossible to achieve if the buccal area is tense because that way it loses much of his sensitivity. Not to say that too much roughness while kissing may end up looking more like a fight between mouths than an erotic and sensual contact.

On the other hand, flexibility gives greater possibilities of contact. This is because a flexible mouth and tongue usually have mobility and an ability to touch diverse points that otherwise would be impossible to approach if your mouth is stiff. But to have and maintain an agile and relaxed buccal area is not enough to remember it at the time of the love encounter. It must be executed through regular practice in order to achieve it. Some ways to do this are the following:

- Practice self-massage on the face daily, especially in the lips and the surrounding area.

- Yawning, moving, and twisting the mouth from right to left next to the swelling of the cheeks as if you were blowing is a good exercise to mobilize the lips.

- Alternately pronounce the letters "O" (pushing the lips as further as possible) and the letter "I" (opening the mouth as much as possible).

Other Kisses Alternatives

When there is a strong attraction and true trust among lovers, kiss variations become practically infinite. There is always a body part to be kissed, a new tongue and lip movement, or a different ways of stimulating your partner. Some ways to achieve greater variety in kisses are the following:

Tasty Kisses

The sense of taste plays an extremely important role in everything related to what's erotic. Kissing is also quite true in this sense. By that, you can add to the kisses a touch of a pleasant flavor. This can result in a pleasant and enhanced experience. To do this, drink or place in your mouth a little bit of a delicious flavor. This can be coffee, some spirits, and so on. An extremely interesting variation is to do it with something that (in addition to have a nice taste) has aphrodisiac effects, such as ginger, dark chocolate, a cinnamon stick, the pulp of a juicy fig, etc. Thermal Kisses

Another possibility is to add the variable of temperature to the kiss between lovers. In this case, as is you might had guesses already, the variables are two: cold and heat. To experience with the first case, a spoonful of crushed ice should be placed in the mouth of the person who is going to give the kiss as soon as the ice melts. In the second, you should drink some very hot beverage and immediately afterward, give the kiss. Of course, if the liquid ingested is tasty, another stimulus will also be added. Be careful when using something hot that it's not too hot so as to burn your partner.

Tantra's kisses

In the oldest texts of tantric sex, five types of kisses are mentioned.

- Puffs: a subtle and unknown technique for many in the West. It's about blowing (especially the neck and mouth area) in order to wake up and enliven the couple's desire.

- Love bite: bite gently the lips and surrounding areas.

- Lingual kiss: this is usually the most frequent kiss among people who are looking for erotic intimacy. In it, tongues touch each other and as well as the lips touching. It's a kind of kiss that awakens genital energy almost immediately.

- Suction kiss: this is also very frequent among lovers. It has two basic variants. In one of them, the upper and lower lips are involved, and suction is exercised on them. The other option is to put both mouths together while they're open and suck the tongue from the partner to your own mouth.

- Soft Lip kiss: while a less "intense" than the previous ones, this kiss isn't that less important. This one is about gently touching the lips with yours.

The kisses of the Kama Sutra

The Kama Sutra can be considered some kind of "ally" of Tantric sex insofar as its sexual techniques are of great help in order to enjoy the moment and our lover's body and spirit during maithuna. Of course, a component that is as important as erotic kissing has its place in the Kama Sutra and Tantric texts. Kama Sutra identify the following as the main types of kisses:

- Nominal kiss: the lips of the lovers touch each other gently without doing nothing else.

- Throbbing kiss: in Indian culture when a young woman wishes to leave shame aside, she wants to touch the lip that presses her mouth. To achieve this, move your lower lip, but not the upper one.

- Touching kiss: this when a woman touches her lover's lip with her tongue and, closing her eyes, and putting her hands in his face.

- Direct kiss: it happens when the lips of the lovers make direct contact and rub each other.

- Inclined kiss: occurs when the head of one of the lovers is up and the other one has it down.

- Rotating or turned kiss: occurs if the lover has his partner's chin in his hand and turns his face to kiss her on the mouth while gently moving the head from side to side.

- Pressure kiss: when lovers kiss while strongly pressing the lower lip

- Great tight kiss: it is practiced having the lower lip between the fingers. Then, after touching it with the tongue, its squeezed very tightly with the lip.

- Kiss of the lower lip: the man kisses the lower lip of the woman. She, in return, kisses his lower lip.

- Oppressor kiss: one of the lovers presses the lips of the other with his/her own lips.

- Tongue combat: one of the lovers plays uses its tongue to play with the teeth, tongue, and palate of the other.

The Kiss of Kisses: Oral Sex

For Tantra, oral sex is the maximum degree of intimacy and contact in relation to kisses. Oral sex for Tantra is when the tongue and lips of one of the lovers touches the genital of the significant other. It is also known as "Buco-genital sex" in the West and has three basic modalities:

- Cunnilingus: the man kisses the yoni.

- Fellatio: the woman has oral contact with the lingam.

- Lovers practice oral sex simultaneously.

Kiss the Yoni

The oral eroticization of the yoni, or cunnilingus, is highly efficient in order to excite a woman and make her enjoy the encounter. Usually it provokes immense pleasure to the receiver. However, the man has to make sure that it's performed constantly while paying attention to the reactions that the woman is having. If all goes well, the man only needs to keep a steady pace and rhythm. If the woman, though, shows signs of discomfort or she's been reluctant or annoyed, it is best to stop or change position. Of course, the greater or lesser degree of humidification is an important signal to know if the woman is actually enjoying the act.

The essential principle of this type of stimulation is to adapt to the individual feminine sensibility. It's extremely important to start smoothly and increase intensity and pressure as time passes by. Something very important to have in account is that although the clitoris is one of the most erogenous zones, applying much pressure to it from the beginning tend to be more annoying and painful than pleasant.

Once it is clear and evident that the woman is excited, the tongue and lips may be more active. A rhythmic and regular touch can serve as a basis, but it is recommended to occasionally modify the movements since monotony could kill off the sexual arousal.

While the clitoris (as we have already pointed out repeatedly) is a nodal point as far as pleasure and desire is concerned, it will be the job of every man to discover which of the areas of this organ reacts better to stimulus. What is more, it's important to realize what moves works best because each woman experiments pleasure differently. Some women need the man to go deeper in order to feel greater pleasure. For others, the external part reacts greatly. The point here is that the man spends some time exploring his lover's body, while the woman helps him in the process.

When the clitoris becomes hard and turgid, it indicates that the woman is feeling aroused and that she's getting closer to have an orgasm. Some forms of cunnilingus are as follows:

- Break through gently separating the labia majora from the vulva with the nose so as to allow the tongue to completely caress the yoni.

- Form circles slowly over the vulva with the nose, lips, and chin.

- Keep the lips of the mouth close to the vulva.

- Gently nibble and suck the clitoris.

- Take the clitoris between your lips.

- When the yoni is already very wet, blow gently, over the vulva and at the entrance of the vagina.

- Form a "U" with the tongue and perform soft and long licks. Start with the clitoris and end at the entrance of the vagina.

- With the tip of your tongue, slowly lick from the perineum to the clitoris.

- Harden the tongue and play with it at the entrance of the vagina.

- Also with a hard tongue, introduce it into the vaginal canal as deep as possible.

- Alternate circular pressures of the tongue on the clitoris with soft suctions in the same organ.

- Get the whole of the clitoris in your mouth.

Kiss the Lingam

Much of what matters the most regarding fellatio is that the man doesn't notice your teeth. At the beginning, it will be convenient to hold the penis with your hand and limit yourself to caress it without having any oral contact. In case the lingam is not yet erected, this friction will help to activate it. If the erection takes time to happen or isn't quite vigorous, the woman can proceed to press both sides of the organ with the lips, without producing a direct contact with the glans. After some time performing this maneuver, the glans and a small part of the phallus will be introduced in the mouth. Then it can be sucked, licked, or even vacuumed.

It is important to take into account that it is convenient to use intervals to prevent that the man from having a premature ejaculation. Some forms of fellatio are the following:

- Form an "O" with the lips and place them carefully over the tip of the lingam. Move your head in tiny circles.

- Allow the glans to slide completely into the mouth and press the trunk firmly between the lips.

- Place your lips as closed as possible to the base of the lingam.

- Gently take the tip of the lingam with your lips while twisting them in a fast way. Kiss the lingam gently and pull the skin back.

- Form a circle with the lips and kiss the entire lingam, sucking and kissing at the same time.

- Tap with the tongue all over the penis, ending in the tip. Hit the glans repeatedly.

- Allow the lingam to penetrate the mouth so deeply as is possible.

Fellatio in the Kama Sutra

This books (which is auxiliary to Tantra) describes the eight basic ways to introduce the lingam into the mouth.

- Nominal union: the lingam is taken by hand, placed between the lips and is rubbed with the mouth.

- Side bite: the lingam is covered with the fingers, while these forms the shape of a flower button. The sides are squeezed with lips, also using the teeth.

- External pressure: the tip of the lingam is compressed with contracted lips, while the woman kisses it as if she wanted to tear it away.

- Internal pressure: the lingam is inserted into the mouth. She squeezes with her lips and then lets it out.

- Kiss: she takes it with one hand and kisses it as if she was kissing the lower lip.

- Polishing: it is caressed everywhere with the tongue—taking care of the tip.

- Suction of the handle: half of the member is introduced into the mouth, while kissing it and sucking it hard.

- Absorption: the lingam is completely introduced into the mouth and compress at the base of it as if was to be swallowed.

Mutual Oral Sex

According to Tantrism, mutual oral sex provides many other advantages in addition to satisfaction and pleasure. To mention few of them, it empowers the sexual center of both lovers, awakens transcendent capabilities, generates a circuit of special energy that contributes to harmonize the vital elements of body and allows sharing of sacred fluids.

One of the most widespread and pleasant positions to do this is by inverting the body with that of the couple. While the man sucks the clitoris or introduces and removes his tongue from the Yoni, the woman can suck and the lingam, as well as caress the testicles. In the West, this position is better known as the "69."

Chapter 7: Positions in Tantric

Although there is no strict formula for sexual positions, several Tantric sources advise the following:

- When the man enters his lingam into the yoni, he must do so with voluptuousness and wisely handling the movements of his body. The forward impulses involve various intensities and different depths. Therefore, performing these movements without been mindful of the body is a sign of lack of understanding of how maithuna works.

- It's convenient to start with small movements and only introducing the tip of the lingam. Repeat this movement with frequency, smoothly and at different intervals.

- When the yoni gets more wet and the woman shows signs of that her excitement is increasing, the lingam should be introduced even deeper, alternating soft and slow movements with sharper ones.

- Before continuing with a deeper penetration, the man will take his lingam with his hand and spin it around the entrance of the yoni.

- After these circular movements, it is convenient that the man takes a break to delay ejaculation and then restart the penetrations. This should be done by combining slow moves with more abrupt and fast ones. It's important to always avoid reaching the bottom of your partner's yoni.

- Then another intermediate period will occur during which the man can perform a series of circular movements around to the entrance of the yoni and rub his lingam in the upper and lower parts of its female counterpart. You must prevent the lingam from penetrating beyond the glans. Likewise, exercise external pressure on the lateral part of the yoni.

- Throughout all this, it is essential that the couple kisses deeply.

- Then, the man will make move in a more direct fashion and perform a deeper penetration, but with episodic outputs of the lingam when he feels the slightest chance of ejaculating.

Penetration Positions

While the conventional position is with woman below, man above, and both lying face to face (also known as missionary) the possibilities of performing this position are truly multiple. There are several ways to link the bodies in an erotic hug. Of course, tantric discipline has taken care of this, similarly to the Indian "Kama Sutra" and the Chinese book of sex and love "Tao."

Some positions allow the women to "master" the rhythm and the speed of the sexual act while others grant more power of movement to the man. Some allow a penetration that is truly deep, and others only allow a more superficial penetration. Some positions make possible a very intimate contact of a good part of the lovers' body, while others only produce contact between the genitals and the surrounding areas. Some facilitate ejaculation and others (on the contrary) help to control it. Next, we detail a series of positions. Purushayata

The man stands with his legs open, leaning on the arms, and the woman sits on him. The advantages of this position lie in the fact that the woman has the initiative of the movements. On the other hand, the man can relax without fear of ejaculating.

Lotus Purushayata

Similar to the previous one, the difference lies in the fact that the man adopts a lotus pose and the woman hugs him with her legs. In this position, blood supply decreases in the lower area of the body (which it includes the sexual organs) and (therefore) is beneficial in order to delay ejaculation. The Two Phases of the Rainbow

This movement consists of two parts. The woman lies on the legs of the man, who lays on his back and joins his chest with his partner's chest. Then, she goes back, so to lay her back on the male legs.

Sukhasana

The man crosses his legs in a lotus pose and receives his partner who has crossed-shaped leg. This is a position that allows full contact as well as allowing the bodies to look at each other. This position results in an intense feeling of fullness and containment.

Sukhasana Variant (on a chair)

The man sits on a chair and the woman sits on him. This variation of the previous position is more suitable for those couples with less physical flexibility. The Elephant

The woman stands and opens her legs, letting her trunk fall until she touches the ground with her hands. The man who's also standing, stands behind her and takes her by the waist performing slow movements. Due to the lack of tension involved, it is a very conducive posture to delay ejaculation.

The Vine

The man and the woman stand and the woman embraces the man with one of her legs.

The Rave

The woman lies on her back and while the man is above her. Meanwhile, she lifts her legs so that her ankles touch the shoulders of her partner. This position allows a very deep penetration.

The Rescue

The woman kneels with her legs open and her back gently curved. The man penetrates her from behind keeping her column straight. It is an extremely pleasant posture that allows strong and dynamic movements. However, it makes it difficult to control ejaculation, given that it slightly tightens the testicles.

Navigating the River

This is a lateral posture in which the woman embraces the man with her arms and legs. This position allows a break from dynamic movements and can immobilize the lovers. This position reproduces a soft wiggle, which is similar to that of a boat sailing on a quiet river.

The Powerful Woman

The man is placed in his back while flexing his legs. The woman sits on the lingam, supporting the buttocks on her legs partner. In this position, the woman can move freely and easily. This position is especially conducive to achieve chain orgasms.

Horse

The man sits and leans on his arms and his partner stands on him. Meanwhile, she's resting her buttocks on his partner's abdomen. The horse is similar to the previous position, since it allows women ample freedom of movement, therefore, promoting female chain orgasms. The Fish

The man stands in supine position and the woman sits on his lingam. She turns her back toward her partner. The man uses his hands and rests close to the shoulders of his partner, while he stimulates her clitoris.

The Sailboat

The woman sits on the man with his back laying down and supports his feet on the floor. This allows the women considerable freedom to move.

The Swing

The woman, lying in her back, raises her legs while the man penetrates her.

The Crab

The woman lies on her back and opens her legs flexing the knees while the man kneels in front of her. The Flight of the Eagle

The man stands on the woman who is lying on her back with the legs intertwined in the buttocks of her partner. This is a posture that allows deep penetration. The Mountain

The woman stands supine with her legs bent over her chest. The soles of her feet should be over the abdomen or chest of her partner. This position also allows a deep penetration. The Sustained Goddess

The woman lies on her back while lying in a supine position. The man kneels in front of her, raising her legs in such a way that places her heels are on his shoulders and neck. The Pyramid

The woman stands on the man with her legs open and turning her back. Meanwhile, he holds her by her thighs with his arms and hands.

The Moon and the Sun

The woman stands on her side and the man does the same from behind. The legs are together and collected to press the lingam. This allows a slow and deep penetration. The Meeting of the Sacred Point

The woman lies on her back and in that position kneels. Meanwhile the man (also kneeling) penetrates her from behind. This allows a deep penetration. Therefore, it's difficult to delay the ejaculation.

The Union of the Fires

The woman lies supine with her legs relaxed and the man stands on her with open legs. His knees and calves should be resting on the floor.

The Dragon

The woman lies on her back. Her partner is in an identical position and lying on her.

Fish vs. Fish

The woman is placed supine and places one leg on the top of the man while with the other she hugs one leg of him. The Bride of Desire

The woman lies on her back, bending her knees up and resting her feet on the ground, raising up her hips. Her partner stands on it and rises while resting his hands on the ground. This posture allows women to perform pelvic movements.

The Mare Runs Wild

Sitting on a chair or armchair, the woman stands with her back facing the man, who delights himself with his partner's breasts. It allows women freedom of movement, especially with regard to the angle at which she's placed. The Love Table

The woman lies supine on a table and flexes her legs open. Meanwhile, the man stands in front of her.

The Big Jump

The man stands up and the woman hugs him with her legs while he holds her by the legs.

Challenging the Universe

The woman places her hands on the floor and raises her legs to reach the hips of the man. The woman must do this while standing in front of him, while the man holds her with his hands on her legs.

Chakrasana

The man is placed in a curved way. He rests with his hands and feet on the floor. Using his own strength, elevates her hip and chest in such way to form an arch similar to a bridge. The woman sits upon he and (while holding with a resting hand the body of man) takes one of her feet with her hand. The male will remain still and the woman will move slowly.

Notice that in order to perform this posture, it's convenient to have warmed up the muscles of the entire body.

The Yoni During the Maithuna

Beyond of what a woman can perform with her body during penetration, knowing how to use her yoni during penetration will turn her into a kind of loving expert. The opening of the vagina can be controlled by the woman in varying degrees, according to the size and consistency of the lingam.

For example, if you lie on your back, lowering your head until your chin touches your chest, and raise the central part of your body, the vaginal opening will be quite wide. Another way to facilitate difficult positions consists of the woman tending herself on her back while raising her thighs in the right angle and separating them as much as possible.

The man can help with his hands to increase the width. However, if you want the opening to narrow, the woman should direct her thighs toward the abdomen and flex the legs by the knees, resting on the side. There are also two basic vaginal movements to perform during intercourse.

The first of these is the spasmodic contraction of the yoni to tighten strongly the lingam, known as "the pincer." This approach can have various effects. In some cases, it accelerates the male orgasm and triggers a brief and medium intensity orgasm for women.

The second movement, known as "the top," consists of a circular displacement in which the yoni is placed upon the lingam. You can practice it in any position that allows a minimum of mobility. The best time to practice this is while performing positions in which the woman rides on the man while he's lying on his back.

Chapter 8: How to Reach an Orgasm

Also known as "the little death," an orgasm constitutes the climax of erotic sensations. It's the most the highest point of sexual ecstasy. As you'll notice later in this chapter, the female and male orgasms are different. Nevertheless, both are the maximum point of sexual pleasure. In addition to that unique feeling of unparalleled enjoyment, the climax entails a fleeting but powerful revolution for much of your body. During it, the partial block of senses (e.g. sight, heard, etc.) can be experienced by some individuals, even before the orgasm occurs. Eventually, it also produces a momentary loss of awareness at the moment of culminating.

Female Orgasm

The female sexual arousal and orgasm are complex processes that involve several levels: physical, emotional, and mental. From a tantric perspective, orgasms constitute for women some sort of spiritual and cosmic bridge that links her with the divine and with the transcendent. As the woman has her genitals internally, it tends to bring energy inward, or to implode. Therefore, it's capable of recharging her own energy. This is contrary to men, who have their genitals out and always seeks to detonate outside, that is to explode.

What is important to understand is how the female orgasms work and what are the phases of it. What is even more important, the woman needs to identify when she has reached an orgasm and when not. The female orgasm is a series of extremely intense and pleasant contractions that fundamentally affect the vagina and uterus. In most cases, it's a reaction that can extend to the legs, belly, and the rest of the body. The first contractions are the most intense and can occur within a very short rhythm. As the orgasm goes on, the contractions become less intense and may occur more randomly.

In general, it requires more time and slowness than its male counterpart. Most women are multi-orgasmic. This means that they have the ability to climax repeatedly throughout a single sexual intercourse.

Female Orgasm Signs

The female orgasm happens in four phases: excitement, plateau, orgasm, and resolution. It is important to keep in mind that it's a division in a certain way that is theoretical and shouldn't be taken as a strict measurement. This is because it's not entirely probable that the person notices the development of each individual stage in her body. In addition, the amount of time the person is in each phase (and even the order) may vary. What is more, the way in which each individual experiences each stage is a personal matter. This could even change depending on the mood and personality of the woman. Roughly speaking, nevertheless, the feminine signs of each one of the phases are as follows: Excitation phase:

- Vaginal lubrication begins.

- The internal area of the vagina expands.

- The uterus and cervix rise upward.

- The labia majora dilatates and separates itself.

- The labia minora enlarge.

- The clitoris increases in size.

- The nipples may become erect as a result of muscle contractions.

- Breasts increase in size.

Plateau phase
- There is a marked increase of sexual tension.

- The outside area of the vagina swells as a result of the arrival of more blood in the area. As a result, vaginal opening is reduced in size.

- The inside of the vagina becomes inflamed, which may be a little painful.

- Decreases vaginal lubrication, especially if this phase is prolonged too much.

- The clitoris becomes erect and the glans move toward the pubic bone.

- The labia minora darkens and continue to increase in size, which usually causes the labia majora to open, thus, the vaginal opening is more prominent.

- The areola (the pigmented area around the nipples) begins to swell.

- Breasts increase in size.

- The so-called "sexual flush" occurs in several areas of the body, as a result of increased blood flow near the surface of the skin.

- Increase of heart rate.

- Increased sexual tension in the thighs and buttocks.

Orgasmic Phase

- Rhythmic muscle contractions occur in the vagina, the uterus and anus. The first of them are more intense and have a faster pace. The following ones might be less intense and more random.

- The sexual blush becomes even more pronounced and can cover large portions of the body.

- The muscles most of the body contract. Eventually, the whole body may contract.

- Some women expel some fluid from their urethra during orgasm, which is known as "female ejaculation."

- At the peak of the orgasm, the whole body can momentarily become stiff.

Resolution Phase

- If sexual stimulation continues, the woman may experience one or more additional orgasms.

- The vagina and the vaginal opening return to their

previous state.

- The breasts, the labia majora and labia, the clitoris and the uterus return to their normal size, position, and color.

- The clitoris and nipples can be so sensitive that any stimulation can be uncomfortable.

- The sexual blush disappears.

- There can be a lot of sweating and deep breathing.

- The heart beats quickly.

- If orgasm does not occur, the woman experiences all the sensations and modifications corresponding to this last phase, but at a much slower pace. Blood trapped in the pelvic organs (which was not dissipated by orgasmic muscle contractions) can result in a feeling of heaviness and pelvic discomfort.

In women, the arrival to an orgasm is usually the highlight of an extensive process that generally follows certain path. First, sexual arousal begins in the brain in response to thoughts such as fantasies and sexual expectations. Likewise, sexual arousal can be a result of visual stimuli—such as seeing her partner naked. Auditory stimulation also goes along and can be performed by listening to sweet and erotic words. Olfactory stimuli are, likewise, necessary and should be composed by different smells and aromas from the partner's body. Finally, the gustatory sense must be explored in order to complete this entire process.

Clitoral and Vaginal Orgasm

Today, and after long controversies that lasted decades, it's now widely accepted that there's no female orgasm without the intervention of the clitoris. It may be surprising, but two-thirds of the vagina lacks nerve endings. Therefore, it makes no sense to talk about different types of orgasms. All orgasms, directly or indirectly, have the clitoris involved somehow. Even women who claim that they can only achieve an orgasm with penetration, they would be surprised to know how they get it. After all, the penis grazes the entrance of the vagina, tapping the pubic bone and making then contact with the clitoris.

Male orgasms

When the sexual arousal phase is prolonged long enough, it triggers the orgasmic phase, which is produced by the reflex contraction of the genital muscles. However, when talking about the male orgasm and about the way it's understood from a tantric perspective, we should first discuss how a male orgasm occurs.

Basically, this happens in two phases. In the first one, the so-called "ejaculatory inevitability" occurs in the internal organs, which consists of the contraction of the internal muscles that drive the fluid from the seminal vesicles and the prostate to the posterior urethra. During this stage, the male perceives a very particular sensation that announces the achievement of an orgasm and ejaculation.

Immediately afterward, and as a second phase, this process is followed by the expulsion of semen through the urethra, along with the contraction of the base muscles of the penis. At the time of the orgasmic emission, the semen goes out through the urinary opening with greater force in young men. After the last penile contractions, the blood that circulates through it is removed venously.

It is usually a common thin (especially among Westerners, since that the Eastern conception differs and quite a bit) to affirm that the sensation of pleasure varies according to the amount of semen emitted. However, this is not the case anymore when taking into account other variables of pleasure. Multiple other factors include psychological conditions of the moment, the type of relations between lovers (a stable couple may experience differently in comparison with occasional relationships), how relaxed the lovers are, etc.

Male Orgasm in Tantric Sex

From the tantric viewpoint of sexuality and eroticism, it results extremely important that the man doesn't ejaculate every time they have a sexual encounter. Ideally, they should only experience one orgasms every ten encounters. This might seem strange at first, but it's important to understand in detail why ejaculation is often avoided:

- First and foremost, Tantra believes that semen is not any type of body fluid. This liquid is a source of energy and creativity by itself. Therefore, each ejaculation implies a loss for man. Either of one or both capabilities. Therefore, there's no point in ejaculating during every sexual encounter.

- Tantra also considers that ejaculations that happen too frequently lead to physical decay, physical decrepitude, and premature aging. "Saving" the semen becomes a kind of guarantee of longevity and of quality of life.

- When the man manages to avoid ejaculation, he can transmute the seminal explosion into an orgasmic implosion so that carnal becomes more of a spiritual experience.

- The fourth determining factor is the fact that once a man ejaculates in a certain moment of sexual intercourse, he loses his erection in his penis. Often, interest is also lost to continue with any type of body contact. Therefore, delaying ejaculation is an excellent practice if you want to ensure feminine satisfaction. Specifically because the women takes longer to get excited and to being predisposed to the sexual act, it also usually requires of more time to reach the climax.

What is more, all men are acquainted with the feeling of desolation that follows ejaculation. After expelling semen, most of the males feel literally surrendered, especially if they ejaculate often. Ejaculation is not necessary, and avoiding it can prolong the sexual act for hours without the desire of ever finishing it. How to achieve that? Tantra offers multiple techniques for that man can delay the emission of semen.

Brahmacharya: Sex Without Ejaculation

Brahmacharya is the sexual act without ejaculation. Likewise, men who have been able to master this skill are called by the same name, which means "Master Brahma." Within Tantric sex, Brahmacharya is a skill that confers great potential on the men who learn it because it allows the man to transmute the seminal energy into spiritual energy. In this way, the sexual act sexual is taken from a simple physical dimension to a more magical and spiritual ceremony.

There are techniques for controlling ejaculation. Tantra recommends making love regularly but without losing energy — i.e. without spilling semen. Eastern disciplines offer a whole range of techniques in order to be capable of doing that. Before starting to discuss each of them further, you need to consider that the first step for achieving this is to remain very calm throughout the encounter. Especially when the man feels the first signs of experiencing and orgasms, as well as during the beginning of it.

One of the most common technique is the one regarding the Hara. In India, the Hara is the muscular center found in the lower belly. When a man concentrates his mind on this body part and places his center of gravity in it, it facilitates the retention of Kundalini energy. In order to do this, you must get under your belly and try to contract the Hara. When doing this, is quite important that you exhale and inhale deeply.

The Prostate Technique

Alternatively, you can use the prostate technique, which consists of giving a little push to the external part of the prostate. In this way, you'll decrease the sensation which is provoked when ejaculation. Therefore, you could immediately inhibit it. The way to do this is by making pressure with one or two fingers on the midpoint between the anus and the upper back, which should be exact opposite side of the testicular bags.

The Testicular Technique

This technique doesn't require you to act upon the testicle itself but on the scrotum. To do this, the man or his partner you should firmly grab the lower part of the scrotum and pull it down as fast as possible.

The Respiratory Method

When man feels that he's about to ejaculate, he must take a slow and deep breath through the nose, followed by an exhalation even slower. Then, keeping he should keep his mouth well closed, will exert slight bit the top of his tongue with his frontal teeth. The idea of this technique is to divert the attention provoked by erotic sensations toward body parts which don't experience much sexual arousal.

Variations of the Previous Method

This is another way of diverting the attention caused by erotic sensations and (more specifically) from the genitals. In order to perform it, simply squeeze your fingers to the point of experiencing pain. Therefore, rub them vigorously to the point that distracts your attention.

The Penis Compression Technique

This technique consists of a compression that is performed at the base of the glans. In order to do it, the man or his partner should hold it between his thumb and forefinger. In such a way, it causes an inhibition of the ejaculatory process.

Asvini Mudra

If ejaculation seems to be imminent, perform several deep breaths while contracting and relaxing the anal sphincter.

Mulha Bandha

Another technique is called Mulha Bandha and consists of contracting the muscles of the anus. When man is closed to have an ejaculation, he simply needs to distend them completely. Afterward, the man should continue contracting and distending such muscles.

Some other techniques to delay ejaculation are:

- Penetrate while counting until nine and then pause counting until nine.

- Perform three soft penetrations for each deep penetration.

- Press on the voluptuous part just below the penis, which will the process of spilling semen and return it to the inside of the body.

- If an orgasm seems imminent, press the tongue to the palate with force.

- Strong tension in the buttocks, abdominal muscles, and those of the lower back is an indication of that ejaculation is just about to happen. To delay and prevent it (in addition to controlling the breathing) the man needs to relax those muscles.

The Help of a Woman

After practicing for a while and becoming self-aware of his body, a man can alone can delay ejaculation with the techniques just explained. However, it's also true that his partner can help to avoid ejaculation. In order to achieve this, it's necessary that the woman is aware of what happens to her lover in the moments just before an orgasm and. Therefore, she should be able to perform some further methods when she detects all of these signs.

- The basic principle that women must take into account in order to delay ejaculation of her partner is to stop or slow down the genital excitation of man. In those moments, the woman must suspend any strong form of stimulation and collaborate with her partner as much as possible.

- It's also essential that at that time, the attention is diverted away from the genital area. One way to do this is by words that distract the attention of the male until he manages to have situation under control again. Another possible way to do this is by performing caresses on areas far from the genitals: feet, hands, calves, etc.

- The woman should be very careful not to perform vaginal pressures on the lingam. Above all, do not perform rotary movements with the pelvis.

- Paying attention to your partner's legs can also be quite helpful. The sudden increase in arousal will make your legs bend while your body is agitated. In order to avoid this erotic tension, the man will try to stretch his lower limbs and the woman should not resist to this.

- Finally, the woman can pull the corona of the glans. This technique should be carried out after prior and common decision of the couple, and never in a sudden way. After pulling down the testicular bags, this will hinder the rise of the testicles, which is an automatic response to ejaculation.

Although tantric sex makes much emphasis on the control of ejaculation, this shouldn't be considered as the end of the sexual act. Especially if the period of excitement and foreplay is prolonged, the lingam will be able to stay hard even after reaching an orgasm. This will allow the man to continue stimulating the lingam with the yoni for a longer period of time. It's very important to be aware of this, since the erected lingam can help the woman to reach an orgasm if she's already predisposed to it. What is more, she can continue experiencing it even after having one.

The Five Levels of Orgasm in Tantra

Both men and women are born with orgasmic capacities since all human beings can experience a climax. However, many women die without ever having enjoyed it due to multiple repressive factors of various societies. Tantra lists five levels of orgasmic joy, which are sorted in an ascending order:

1.   Preorganic: Kundalini energy is prepared for been distributed. This is an extremely pleasant state, although without reaching an orgasm. However, it's quite common that a couple can't go on to the next level.

2. Occasional: This is a variation of the first. In this case, penetration takes place and pleasant sensations are experienced without been able to reach fully an orgasmic phase. The causes for this can be multiple: emotional or physical tensions, mental blocks originated due to prejudices or false moral ideas, stress caused because of everyday problems, etc.

3. Orgasmic: this is the state in which most people (both women and men) feel satisfied and consider the sexual act over. It is an extremely physical sensation in particular, which is indeed very pleasant. However, it does not go beyond that and doesn't transcend to a further level.

4. Chain orgasms: achieving this can help a couple to feel much fuller. This is relatively common for couples who have been trying tantric sex. In these cases, one orgasm happens after the other.

5. The wave of happiness: this level is common for regular practitioners of tantric sex techniques. In it, orgasms are extremely powerful and extended over time.

Oriental Secrets to Improve Orgasm

As we clarified at the beginning of this chapter, an orgasm is triggered by the reflex contraction of the genital muscles. As any other muscle, these can exercise and strengthen to improve their functionality. Furthermore, it can help you to optimize an orgasm. Because tantric sex preaches that male ejaculation should be spread through time as much as possible, it also provides some hints on how to do this. Ejaculating is not a mere discharge of seminal fluid, but some sort of erotic event, which normally is highly pleasurable. Due to all the aforementioned reasons, here are some exercises that can help you to improve this experience.

- Focus attention on the pelvic muscles. Contract the buttocks and simulate as if you're to urinate. Contain yourself by squeezing the pelvic muscles so as to prevent the imaginary stream of urination from coming out.

- Contract the pelvic muscles for about fifteen minutes, three times a day.

- When urinating, interrupt the stream as many times as possible.

- The rigidity of the lingam can be increased by placing a cloth, usually a towel, on the erected limb. The duration of this exercise and the amount of weight supported must be increased progressively. Be careful of not overdoing it and improve slowly.

The Ghost of Helplessness

What is generically known as "impotence" is (in reality) a range of phenomena of a somewhat diverse nature with a common issue; the lack of penile erection. There are different variants of it, such as:

- The man can never achieve an erection.

- The erection is achieved but disappears as soon penetration happens.

- The erection is achieved and maintained before and during penetration, but disappears before the man can experience an orgasm.

There are several alternatives to tackle this issue. For one, do not make the serious mistake of thinking that you can't start making love until you have a full erection. Sex is not synonymous with carnal penetration. Sexual intercourse covers a huge amount of pleasant practices that do not involve explicit intercourse. Focusing entirely on penetration is a great obstacle for men who can't relax and enjoy the moment. For the most part, this can prevent them to have a full erection. Therefore, the second fundamental step is to relax.

Contrary to what one might think, stimulation is not all what a man needs in order to have an erection. Thus, relaxing is fundamental for this purpose. It may bring you calm and allow you to enjoy your feelings. Any tension that is not conveniently oriented toward the progressive development of the sexual act has a certain inhibitory effect. If you have an erection, it is best to devote yourself to the excitement of your partner. What is more, when you notice signs of pleasure, it is very likely that (at a conscious level) your start to feel much more desirable.

The Flaccid Erection Problem

Sometimes it happens that an erection does not go away completely, but the lingam does not erect completely. This is commonly known as "flaccid erection." Some things can be done in this sense. As mentioned before, it's not worth making the mistake to think that making love is just a mere insight of a penis that is perfectly erect. First and foremost, relax and get rid of negative fantasies. Some principles of tantric sex provide some advice about this:

- A lingam with a flaccid erection can be introduced and without excessive difficulty when female lubrication is considerable. What may prevent penile penetration is the pressure of the vaginal walls. In this sense, it will be necessary to perform a sexual position that doesn't provoke so much pressure to the penis—e.g. sidewise.

- Another technique (which doesn't exclude the previous one) is that the woman or man hold the glans with two fingers and insert it partially into the vagina.

- Form a ring with your fingers and compress with it using a slight pressure on the back of the penis. This helps not to lose an erection when obtained.

- Once relative rigidity of the lingam is achieved, it is essential to complete and maintain it by reciprocating movements. In addition, these will have the additional advantage of fueling the excitation of the woman. Bear in mind that such approach, as explained before, is a crucial way to stimulate both of the partners.

- After this short phase, it is possible that there is no more need to permanently put pressure on the penis by placing the fingers at its base. Lovers, however, must remain vigilant about it to perform again that technique if necessary.

Simultaneous Orgasm

It's important to demystify the search for simultaneous orgasm. This is a goal that often times is useless. Furthermore, is leads only to add frustration and a sense of failure to what is considered as a poor imitation of a good sexual relationship. Unfortunately, there are many couples who spend their sex time trying to retain or speed up orgasms in order to end together. For both men and women, this tension can generate a lot of stress and discomfort. Consequently, sexual arousal can fade away slowly.

When you feel that you and your partner will reach an orgasm at the same time, the feeling is very pleasant. However, the truth is that the orgasm is a lonely experience and is quite hard to realize exactly what is happening on the inside and outside. Furthermore, it would be close to impossible to observe how your partner is enjoying the moment if the climax is simultaneous.

Conclusion: Final Recommendations and Thoughts

The secret of tantric sex lies in the techniques that we discussed during this book. However, be mindful that tantric sex not only has the goal of prolonging the sexual ecstasy and making your encounters more satisfactory, but to help you to connect in deeper levels with your partner. Keep in mind that Tantra expects you to have the interests and desires of your partner at heart.

Tantric sex and love is all about caring. One of the reason why there's much "emptiness" in the modern relationships is selfishness and egocentrism. In this very sense, tantra is some sort of cure. Tantra attempts to unify people. Tantric principles are nothing but a way to become more considerate and compassionate individuals.

Tantra is something to be incorporated into your life. One of the most significant outcomes of doing so is feeling more in touch with what happens around you. What is more, the relationship with your partner will be enhanced.

So, before finishing I'll like to share with you some final recommendations for practicing Tantric Sex.

1. Maintain eye contact with your partner at all times. It's said that eyes are the place where the soul is mirrored. Therefore, looking to your partner's eyes during maithuna can lead to the most intense sexual experiences. One of the fastest ways to increase your sexual pleasure is to look your partner in the eye. Do this in order to figure out how he/she's feeling. Pay attention to it as use it as a guide.

Concentrate on your thoughts and try to use your eyes as a way to communicate with your partner. It doesn't matter at what point of the encounter are you, make sure that there's eye contact at all moment.

What is more, I recommend you not to lose it (especially) when having a reach orgasm. If you manage to do this, the experience will be extraordinary.

2. Feel every pore of your and your partner's skin. As mentioned throughout the book, feeling each other bodies is a key factor in maithuna. One of the most important points of it is to explore the sensuality of your partner through games, dances and caresses. Tantric sex focuses on feeling the touch of the other person. As mentioned in Chapter 6, an orgasm can be achieved even without penetration. In order to do so,

you must be totally focused on what you are doing. Try not to think about things other than what's happen here and now. Your partner has to be the center of attention.

At all moments, you should know what your partner wishes and expects. Therefore, you should make sure to fulfill those expectative. You should be aware of the areas of the body that you're touching. As well, don't forget to pay attention to the way your partner is reacting. Behind every move and touch, there should be a purpose. As we mentioned several times throughout the book, if you're aware of how to use your body you'll then have a complete repertoire to apply on your partner.

3. Be aware of your senses during maithuna. Tantric sex isn't only a physical experience. It also involves the emotional and psychological aspects of sexuality. Thus, your smell, sight, touch, hearing and taste are all involved in the encounter. Therefore, it's very important that you and your partner explore the sensations that you are creating in your body, as well as the body of your partner.

Pay attention in the natural ways in which your senses react. Don't forget to always create a relaxed and intimate atmosphere. This way, it will be possible to achieve a sexual experience that will be more fulfilling. Think about how each of your senses are been boosted. Practice some of the many ideas that I shared with you in the past chapters.

A simple but efficient way to improve your sexual life is by making small changes –particularly in how your senses are engaged. If you feel that your sexual life is missing something, it's highly likely that it's related to your senses. Sex and making love are (foremost) sensorial experiences. Thus, make the most of your encounters by stimulating your senses. Furthermore, you might have a sense that is more sensible than others. If so, make your mission discover which of your sense is.

4. Make sure that you experience orgasms with your whole body. An advantage of tantric sex is that you can experience an orgasm with your whole body. While it might sound strange, there's a way to arouse all of your body parts. One of the ways to achieve this type of orgasm is to practice maithuna while engaging the Kundalini energy. This keeps you close to the climax and let it then fade away little by little.

Therefore, remember that an orgasm is first achieved due to things like foreplay. You must practice it constantly in order to reach the climax. As we discussed before, use your breathing and the power of your impulses to spread energy through your partner's body. Keep a constant tension and used the techniques exposed before to prevent ejaculating. However, keep your partner and yourself near to an orgasm. When you finally reach orgasm, you will feel strong and pleasant contractions in different parts of your body.

Take into account that tantric sex helps you to use all of your body when making love. There's a strong fixation over genitals. Regularly, people only think about them regarding sex. That's the exact formula for unpleasant and/or incomplete sex.

5. Finally, the most important thing is that you enjoy the experience. Tantric sex isn't just a mean to reach an orgasm and prolonged it as much as possible. What matters the most is the process to achieve that. This entire journey requires that you focus on exploring your partner and creating a beautiful atmosphere. Thus, stop thinking about the end. This way you'll be able to achieve a higher level of satisfaction in your relationship.

Sometimes we put too much emphasis on the end result—often to reach an orgasm. Many times, we neglect the fun and pleasure caused by the way we take in order to reach that goal. Tantric sex makes an special emphasis in enjoying the process of becoming better. Thus, don't focus entirely on the outcomes. Make sure that the experience of learning and applying tantra is joyful for you and your partner.

If you are constantly chasing the possibility of climaxing, you and your partner will end up not enjoying the experience at all. Remember that hurrying is an enemy of maithuna. Don't think entirely about the orgasm. Think about the entire process in a holistic way. In this book, you've found several ideas and techniques to trigger your sexual life. You don't need to put them all in practice. Cherry pick those who seem more interesting to you and experiment with them

A key aspect of tantric sex is experimentation. Therefore, try new things. The rest will come naturally. Maithuna isn't something that you can plan beforehand. While its principles are crucial, take them as a starting point and go ahead. Try using the foods described before, the different positions, and the dances and rituals. Furthermore, Tantra isn't in conflict with other approaches to sex. Therefore, continue looking for new philosophies and approaches. Tantra is completely compatible with many of them.

Also, make certain that your partner (or partners) are agreeable to trying the techniques mentioned in this book. You don't want to do anything to upset your partner or that would disrupt your lovemaking. You need to be upfront and trusting of each other.

Don't rush into any of the described techniques before you are ready, and don't sweat it if the first time or two, things don't go as you planned. Experimentation will help you to master the tantric techniques.

And don't forget to try the recipes that are included in this book. Not only are they tasty, but they will serve as an entree to your sexual experience.

Last but not least, I hope that you're making the most of this book. It's prime and overall intention is to provide you with elements that can improve your sexual life as well as the relationship with your partner. If you've enjoyed this book, make sure to share it with somebody who might make good use of it.

I wish you the best in this exciting journey! Remember that this is only the beginning. Walk toward your goal without forgetting to enjoy the path you're walking!